A YEAR'S CAMPAIGNING IN INDIA

A YEAR'S CAMPAIGNING IN INDIA

FROM MARCH, 1857. TO MARCH, 1858

By

JULIUS GEORGE MEDLEY

GYAN

Published by

GYAN

Gyan Publishing House
5, Ansari Road
Daryaganj, New Delhi-110002
Phone: 011-47034999, 9811692060
E-mail: books@gyanbooks.com

Distribution Network
gyanbooks.com
India, USA, Canada, UK, Australia, France

ISBN : 978-81-212-6496-9 (PB)
First Published, 1858

2nd Impression 2022

Printed at: Gyan Press, Delhi.

A YEAR'S CAMPAIGNING IN INDIA
Author: JULIUS GEORGE MEDLEY

FROM A PHOTOGRAPH — MACLURE MACDONALD & MACGREGOR, LONDON

NATIVE OFFICER OF THE PUNJAB PIONEERS.

A MUZBEE SIKH.

PUBLISHED BY W THACKER & CO LONDON, CALCUTTA & BOMBAY

A YEAR'S CAMPAIGNING IN INDIA,

FROM MARCH, 1857. TO MARCH, 1858.

By JULIUS GEORGE MEDLEY,

Captain Bengal Engineers, and Garrison Engineer of Lucknow.

WITH PLANS OF THE MILITARY OPERATIONS.

"We are but warriors for the working day,
Our gayness and our gilt are all besmirch'd
With rainy marching in the painful field,
But, by the mass, our hearts are in the trim."

"Once more unto the breach, dear friends, once more,
Or close the wall up with our English dead!"

King Henry V.

1858.

To A. C. S.

I DEDICATE THESE RECORDS OF THE YEAR

THAT FIRST MADE US ACQUAINTED.

PREFACE.

THE following pages, written primarily for the perusal of friends and relatives in England, may, it is hoped, be found sufficiently interesting to the general reader to excuse their publication in the present form, containing, as they do, a personal narrative of several of the most important events in the late (or, rather, present) wars in India, which have absorbed so much interest amongst Englishmen in general.

In a personal narrative of this sort, it is difficult to give enough individual interest to the description, without being too egotistical, or imagining that all the world is concerned in one's own petty share in important events. I have endeavoured to keep this medium, but would beg the reader to bear in mind that I am not professing to write a history of the campaign, but simply a popular account of a subaltern's share in it.

The narrative embraces an account of the Bozdar Expedition in the Derajat Hills, in March, 1857;

the Siege and Capture of Delhi, in September, 1857; Colonel Seaton's Campaign in the Doab, in December of the same year; and the Siege and Capture of Lucknow, in March, 1858.

The first of these has nothing to do with the war of the mutinies, but I have introduced it partly because it is included in the "Year's Campaigning," dating backwards from the Capture of Lucknow—the last operation in which I took part; and partly because it will give the reader some idea of the peculiarities of the frontier warfare, which has been a great school of officers for India in her late hour of need, and which trained the only portion of the Bengal Native Army that, as a body, remained true to their salt, and have done such splendid service to Government in the late campaign.

If I have enlarged principally on the services of the Engineers in this war, it is only because I myself am an Engineer, and not from any wish to detract from the splendid services performed by the other branches of the army.

Out of sixty-four officers of the Bengal Engineers actually engaged in the campaign, we lost nine killed and twenty-two wounded, being nearly fifty per cent., besides three others murdered by the rebels.

It was unfortunate for the corps that so few of our officers above the rank of subalterns were engaged; so that the strict rule of the service, requiring the rank of Captain to be obtained by seniority, before any promotion can be given for services in the field, has prevented us having much share in the brevets and decorations so liberally bestowed. It is still more unfortunate for a corps like the Engineers, as I may venture to say, without fear of contradiction, that the duties of a subaltern of Engineers in the field, but more especially at a siege, involve far more work and responsibility than usually fall to the lot of that grade in the other branches of the army; and from the slowness of promotion in our corps, we had the mortification of finding ourselves continually superseded by our juniors in the Royal Engineers, when the two corps met at Lucknow and elsewhere. That this, however, will be remedied when once drawn to the notice of Government, I have no manner of doubt.

LUCKNOW,
July 19th, 1858.

CONTENTS.

LIST OF ILLUSTRATIONS.

A YEAR'S CAMPAIGNING IN INDIA.

CHAPTER I.

THE BOZDAR EXPEDITION.

THE Western frontier of the Punjab is but little known out of that province, and is a *terra incognita* to very many in it. A narrow strip of land between the Indus and the Suleiman range of mountains extends from the hills and valleys of the Kohat district to the Scinde frontier, and is known for two-thirds of its length by the name of the Derajat. The aspect of this country is peculiar. A thin fringe of cultivation and jungle extends along the bank of the great river, and terminates, as you advance into the interior, in a flat, desert country, where a precarious supply of water from the hills affords a poor cultivation in the vicinity of the thinly scattered villages. As you get lower down, the hill streams become smaller, and the aspect of desolation still greater, so that you may ride for miles without seeing a human being, and unable to procure a drop of water to relieve the thirst engendered by the heat of these scorching plains. The Puthan and Belooch tribes who inhabit the hills have many of the characteristics of the Highlanders of a century ago as described by Macaulay. The same feudal attachment to their chiefs—the same internal blood feuds descending from father to son—the same incapacity of combining for any fixed purpose—the same difficulty of discerning between the laws of *meum* and *tuum*, and withal a certain martial bearing and innate love of freedom, stamp them as a race quite apart even from the warlike races of Northern India,—and make them a much more interesting people than the cringing and pliant Poorbeah.

The scarcity of water makes cultivation a much greater labour than in more favoured spots, and herds of cattle are reared on the scanty pasturage at the foot of the hills to eke out the subsistence of the hill borderers. Within the chain of barren mountains, however, are fertile patches here and there, which depend on the scanty showers of rain that fall, or on the occasional swelling of the hill torrents. The only roads into the country are the beds of these torrents, covered with boulders brought down by the force of the water, or difficult footpaths across the low hills, known only to the inhabitants. Secure in such an impracticable country, and partly incited by poverty, the hill tribes have from time immemorial made raids on their wealthier neighbours in the plains, and looked upon cattle-lifting as an honourable and gentlemanly pursuit.

Neither Mahomedan nor Seikh ruler ever cared to ask for tax or tribute from these unruly gentry: they were only too well satisfied if they would let their tax-paying subjects alone; and, indeed, paid various sums to different chieftains nominally for the care of the passes and protection of travellers, but really as black mail to keep their marauding propensities under some sort of check.

When the country fell under our rule with the rest of the Punjab, we kept up the same custom, and probably paid them their allowances rather more regularly than they had formerly been accustomed to receive them. But the innate propensities of the race would constantly break out, and we did not wink at infractions of the nominal treaty quite so readily as the Seikhs; so plundering and marauding were carried on with various success on their part, and when we could catch them, they got what they deserved. Taught by three or four years of experience, the general policy of the Government was as follows:—When a particular tribe became troublesome, the allowance (if any) paid to the chief was reduced, or stopped altogether. If this had no effect, they were forbidden the plains, and outlawed. If they still continued to plunder, then the patience of Government became exhausted. An expedition was undertaken against them, they were attacked in their own country, well thrashed and closely pursued, their villages burnt, crops destroyed and cattle seized, and the force usually remained until the chiefs came in and made submission and reparation, and gave hostages for future good behaviour.

The troops holding this long line of frontier were the Punjab Irregular force, consisting entirely of natives, of course under European officers, comprising cavalry, infantry, and artillery, to the number of 12,000 men, drawn from all castes and creeds, and with many of the very men I have been describing in their ranks. Officered by picked men, isolated from the prejudices of the Line army, and trained in this rough school of warfare, involving severe marches, incessant fights, and exposure at all seasons of the year, this force formed a source of strength to which the Government gladly turned when the regular army mutinied; and drawing them from the frontier, sent many regiments into Hindostan, where they fought side by side with the English troops, and behaved with unswerving fidelity from first to last. The names of Chamberlain, Coke, Nicholson, Hodson, Probyn, Watson, Wilde, Green, &c., all highly distinguished in the war with the mutineers, will show the style of officers trained in this school.

The tribes on the lower Derajat frontier had always been much quieter than their northern brethren; but at the beginning of 1857 one tribe had been running up a long score of offences, and the cup of their iniquities was full to overflowing. They had robbed, and burnt, and murdered, and had very rarely been caught. On one occasion they had surprised and cut up one of our temporary military posts, and carried off 800 rupees of Government money. Their allowance had been stopped, and they had been outlawed, but without effect; and at last they became so bad, that it was necessary to move a whole regiment of cavalry out to watch the mouths of the passes leading into their country, to prevent their debouching in force on the plains.

This tribe (the Bozdars) numbered about 2,500 fighting men; they dwelt in the hills opposite Mungrota, some fifty miles north of Dera Ghazee Khan, and had been a troublesome tribe in the time of the celebrated Seikh governor, Sawun Mull. That able man had indeed led an expedition against them; but, though at first successful, he had been pressed so hard in his retreat, that he only escaped by leaving behind all his booty, and more than 200 of his soldiers killed and wounded.

The permission of Government was at length obtained for an expedition to be undertaken against them; and late in February, Brigadier Chamberlain came down to organize the necessary force. I had been stationed in this part of the country for the last four years, residing at Dera Ghazee Khan, and employed partly as a military engineer in charge of the frontier posts, and the two cantonments of Dera Ghazee Khan and Amee, and partly as a civil engineer in charge of the irrigation canals of the district. I was now ordered to accompany the column as field engineer, taking with me a company of Punjab Sappers that was then under me, and a proper engineer equipment of intrenching tools, scaling ladders, powder bags, &c.

On the 5th March I joined the camp then assembled at Tamsa, near Mungrota, and eight miles from the mouth of the pass by which we were to enter the Bozdar country.

The column consisted of the following troops:—

One wing (about 400 men) of the 1st Punjab Infantry (Coke's).

One wing of the 2nd P. I. (Green's).

One wing of the 4th P. I. (Wilde's).

One wing of the 1st Seikh Infantry (Gordon's).

One wing of the 3rd Seikh Infantry (Rennie's).

About 100 Sowars of the 2nd Punjab Cavalry (Browne's), two 9-pounders, and two 24-pounder howitzers, under Lieutenant Sladen.

Eight mountain guns and howitzers under Lieuts. Mecham and Maister, 1st Company Punjab Sappers. The two civil officers, Captains Pollock and Graham, were to accompany us.

No European had ever penetrated into the country before, and our accounts of it were derived solely from native information.* Two passes (those of Mahoee and Mungrota), twelve miles apart at their mouths, led into the interior, and were there connected by a third. Both were difficult, but the latter had sundry advantages in the way of water, forage, &c., which made it the preferable route. Ten miles inside, measuring from the mouth of the Mungrota Pass, was the enemy's strong position, where we knew he had for some time been preparing to make his principal stand. It was the same place where Sawun Mull had been beaten, and the Bozdars were confident in its great strength and supposed impregnability.

* Great credit was given to Captain Graham, the civil officer, for the very correct map of the country he had compiled entirely from information furnished by spies.

On the morning of the 6th, the bugle sounded at 1 a.m., and at 2 o'clock the column was in motion—the advanced guard furnished by the 1st Seikhs, the rear guard from the 4th Punjab Infantry. We marched on to Mungrota, where we picked up the cavalry, halted for the column to close, and then went on to the mouth of the pass over a very rough road. Here we halted again, and waited till day-break, when the column went down into the pass by a steep road I had cut a few days before. I saw the heavy guns safely down, and then rode on to join the Brigadier.

We were now marching along the bed of the Mungrota or Sunghur Nullah, nearly dry during the greater portion of the year, but for the few days when rain falls in these hills, bringing down a formidable stream of water. The bed was sandy, very irregular, and covered with boulders of large size. The road was execrable, but the sturdy little Cabul horses that drew the guns never shirked their work, and took them along admirably, though sixty horse-shoes were lost in this one march.

The width of the pass was about 200 yards on an average, but it varied considerably. It was enclosed on both sides by rugged and barren rocks, often rising up perpendicularly to a height of several hundred feet.

Pickets were sent up on both sides every now and then to take possession of any particular heights which looked suspicious, and whence a good look-out was maintained for the enemy. But not a soul was in sight, and we marched on unmolested, the long column of camels, mules, and tattoos on which the baggage of the force was laden, being closed in by a strong rear guard.

At length we saw three or four men on a distant ridge, who were evidently watching our movements, and who moved on parallel with the head of the column for some time, and then disappeared in advance, to give notice of our approach. Shortly afterwards, the bugles sounded the halt, and we found ourselves in a pretty little recess from the pass, where a flat piece of ground, covered with green wheat and a few trees, was to be the site of our first encampment. These spots are locally termed *kuchees*, and many of them are of several acres in extent, forming picturesque spots amongst the sterility of the surrounding hills.

Our camp was now pitched in the young corn; strong pickets were posted on the neighbouring heights, whence an enemy might have annoyed us; and soon the hammering of tent pegs, as the white tents were quickly raised on all sides, the shrill neighing of horses, the braying of mules, and the groans of the camels, gave indications of our first march being over. Officers and men stretched themselves in the grateful shade, fires were lighted, and breakfast quickly prepared, and over the succeeding cheroots and pipes the probabilities of a fight on the morrow were discussed. Suddenly, a sharp rattle of musketry was heard. All ran out of their tents to ascertain the cause of the firing, and we saw that one of our pickets had been attacked, and was exchanging shots pretty freely with the enemy's matchlockmen. Supports were quickly sent up, and it was interesting to see the men swarming up the steep hills, their figures growing less and less in the distance, and looking like ants toiling to the summit, until they stood on the crest of the ridge, and became visible against the clear blue sky.

The firing soon ceased, the enemy having retired as our supports drew near; and then we found that the Brigadier intended starting at once with a strong reconnoitring party to have a look at the formidable position we had heard so much of, which was to be attacked on the morrow, and which was only three miles ahead of us.

So about 2 p.m. the party left camp, consisting of all the cavalry, and about 500 infantry from Coke's and Rennie's corps. We rode on for about a mile, when two or three shots echoed amongst the hills, and the enemy's look-outs hastened on to their friends to give warning of our being near. Our road still lay through the bed of the Sunghur Nullah, over the boulders of which our horses could hardly go out of a walk. At length we came to a point where a branch nullah (the Droog) ran up to the right, and the enemy's position lay before us.

Both nullahs were shut in by high, precipitous rocks, on the summits of which ran a series of parallel ridges, which were lined by the Bozdars, affording them complete shelter, and enabling them thoroughly to command both passes, with their long matchlocks. Barriers of stones had been thrown across the bed of the nullah at one or two points to check our advance, but these were not very formidable, and small stone field-works, called *sunghurs*, were established on convenient heights, and occupied in force. The Droog Nullah was narrower than the other pass, and the hills on both sides were more precipitous, a sharp turn of the pass to the right giving, moreover, a formidable front fire to be overcome by a force attempting to advance, as well as that on both flanks. The whole position, known as the Khanbund, was truly formidable, and the enemy looked confident and determined to maintain it.

As it was desirable to see to what length the position extended, part of the infantry were here halted, to secure our retreat, and the Brigadier, with his staff and escort of cavalry, rode forward up the principal nullah to inspect it. As soon as they saw our advance, the enemy showed themselves in great force on the ridges on both sides, and opened a very hot fire, saluting us, at the same time, with loud shouts and yells. On we rode, however, for about half a mile, until we found ourselves close to the end of the position, when, having seen all that he wanted, the Brigadier turned his horse, and we all rode back again, as fast as it was possible to get over such bad ground. On seeing us turn, the Bozdars redoubled their yelling, and the fire from the heights increased in severity, the bullets ringing through the air, and striking the stones and rocks around. A Duffadar of police was shot through the heart, and another man was wounded; and, emboldened by the smallness of our force, a party descended from the higher ridge to get nearer to us, and try to cut off our retreat. This was too much of a joke, and Coke's Infantry, who were with us, were ordered to ascend and drive them back. In an instant they were scrambling up the steep hill side, and a sharp interchange of firing took place. The party of the enemy retired as Coke's men advanced, and our Sepoys took possession of a commanding spot, which covered our retreat; but when we had passed, the infantry had to effect their retreat, and, as they descended from their secure situation, the enemy followed them boldly. Our men, however, quite accustomed to this kind of work, retired very deliberately and regained the pass in perfect order, though not without losing two men killed, and three wounded.

We now returned to camp, which we reached in another hour, having well reconnoitred the position, and feeling pretty well convinced that we should have a tough fight on the morrow.

The next morning (the 7th) the bugle sounded at 5 o'clock. No advancing in the dark now. By 6, we were in full march for the enemy. The advance and rear guards were of course strengthened, the cavalry going with the latter, as there was no ground for them to act on. The baggage was in rear of the main body, and the long column of infantry and artillery, baggage, and camp followers, went streaming up the pass, until we came in sight of the enemy's position. Then a halt was called, the baggage was closed up and left under a proper guard in a secure spot, and the Brigadier rode forward with the staff and commanding officers to arrange the plan of attack. I had stayed behind with the Sappers to help the heavy guns over an awful bit of road, which having been safely accomplished, I rode on again to join the Brigadier.

The enemy saw we had come to fight this time, and not merely to look, and they watched our operations in silence, keeping themselves so perfectly concealed behind the ridges, that, except one or two on the look-out, it was impossible to see a single man from below.

The non-military reader will easily understand that the thing to be done was to drive the Bozdars off the hills, as the attempt to pass a large body of men and animals, without "crowning the heights," as it is technically termed, and between two "walls" of fire, would be madness. As there were two nullahs, or passes, the ridges on both sides of which were occupied by the enemy, it is evident that there were four series of heights to be carried, and the attack was ordered by Brigadier Chamberlain to be made as follows:—

Major Gordon, with the 1st Seikh Infantry, was directed to clear the heights on the *left* of the principal pass; these were very steep, but were not held so strongly as the others, being off the enemy's line of retreat.

Captain Wilde, with the 4th Punjab Rifles, was to clear the heights on the *right* of the principal pass (the Sungurh); he was aided by the four heavy guns, which were to play from the pass on the opposite ridges.

Major Coke and Captain Green, with the 1st and 2nd Punjab Infantry, were to attack the minor pass (the Droog), and clear the heights on both sides.

Captain Renny, with the 3rd Seikh Infantry, was at first left in reserve, but afterwards brought up to attack the heights on the *left* beyond Gordon's range.

The mountain guns were to aid Coke and Green, and play upon the ridges of the Droog Nullah.

The enemy had watched our dispositions in perfect quietness; but while the Brigadier was explaining the position from which the heavy guns were first to open, one of their leaders called out to us from the opposite ridge, where he stood with his long matchlock in hand, and white dress and turban shining in the sun. We shouted in reply, and then he asked, "Why don't you come? What are you waiting for? Why did you turn back yesterday?" to which a guide who was with us replied, "Brother, be content—we are coming directly." At length, all being ready, the Brigadier gave the word; a shot from one of the 9-pounders echoing with a grand sound over the hills, gave the signal to the infantry to ascend the heights from the ends of the ridges, where they were drawn up. I was then with the Brigadier at the smaller pass.

A portion of the infantry was lying down in the nullah to assist the artillery in covering the ascent of their comrades to the summit. Hitherto, not a shot had been fired by the enemy; but no sooner had the troops begun to ascend the steep rocks, than a line of white smoke gleamed from the ridge in front, and a shower of bullets fell in the pass. Simultaneously, from every ridge and favourable spot where the enemy lay so well concealed, a sharp, biting fire was poured on the artillery, on the covering party in the nullah, and on the men ascending the heights. Our men, however, swarmed up the hills at a surprising rate. The enemy's fire was sharply returned, as our soldiers advanced, and the hill sides were dotted over with men hardly visible at a distance, except as the puffs of smoke showed the line of attack. Meanwhile, the artillery had been throwing shells with beautiful precision, making them burst just over the ridges, —varied with round shots, which smashed the rocks to atoms, and sent the splinters flying around. The enemy, however, fought hard; they had the vantage ground, and almost all the wounds received by our men were severe, from the direction of the balls which were fired from above. Our wounded were going fast to the rear; but the Sepoys pressed steadily on, and the enemy, seeing us determined

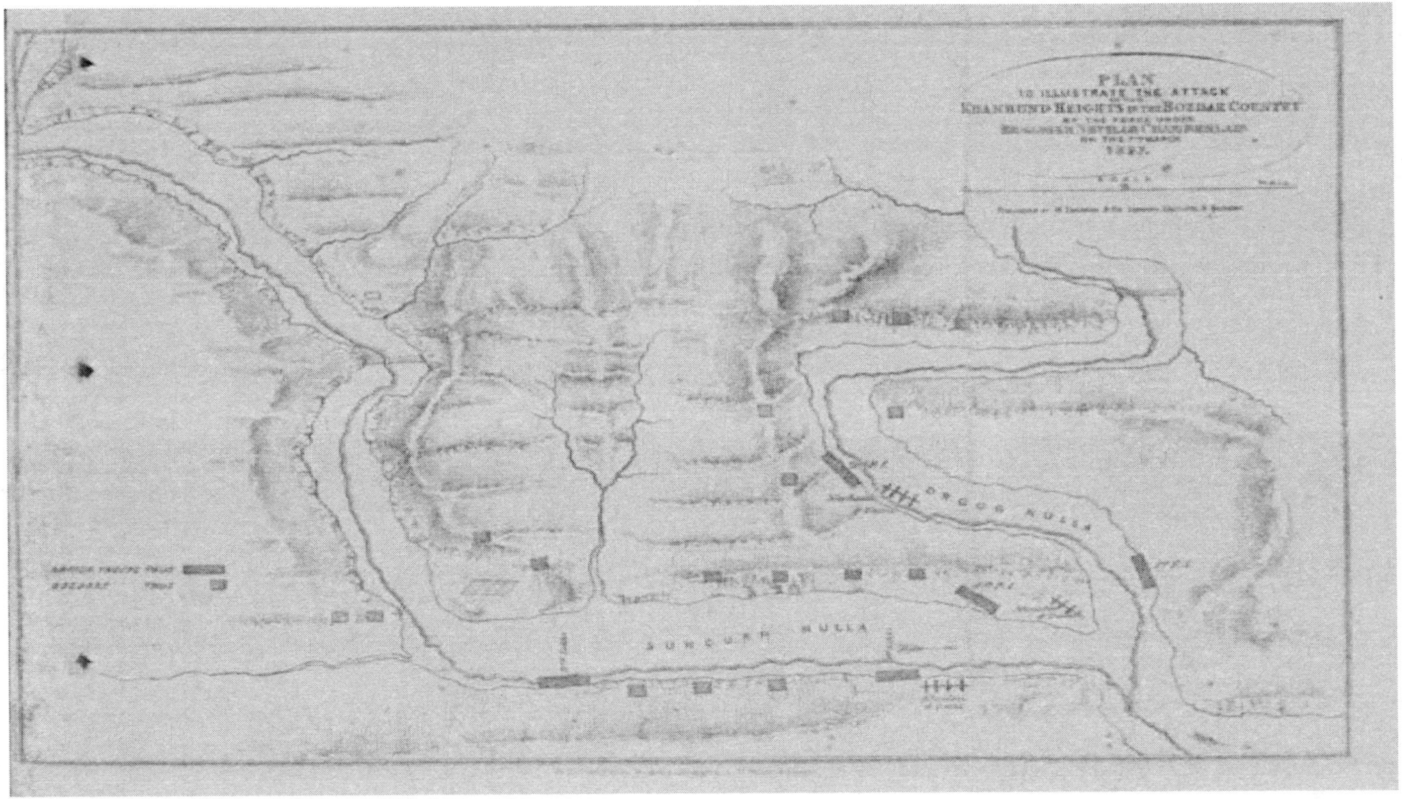
PLAN
TO ILLUSTRATE THE ATTACK
NULLA
NULLA

to close, fell slowly back, still fighting bravely. As he retired, our artillery advanced a little along the nullah, and again unlimbering, pitched the shell and shot as before, keeping well in front of our own infantry, as they pressed on the retreating foe; —for three hours the action lasted in this way, our men steadily gaining position after position, and driving the Bozdars along the ridge. The incessant noise of the musketry, and louder peals of the artillery, had quite a different sound from what would have been heard in the plains; each report was multiplied by a thousand echoes, and the continued reverberation was indescribably grand.

Not being wanted in my own more immediate department, I was doing duty as aide-de-camp to the Brigadier, and rode about, taking orders from one pass to the other, so that I saw the whole fight very well. At length the enemy were forced back right to the end of their position; our troops were everywhere pressing on them, and having gained the highest ridges, were no longer on the worse ground; the Bozdars were driven to their last Sanghurs,—these were shelled by the heavy guns, and then stormed by the 3rd Seikhs, and the enemy fled over the hills in every direction.

The whole position had been carried, and the infantry, having swept the ridges clear of the foe, descended into the pass once more, and encamped a short distance on ahead in the Hurrunbole Kuchee. Our loss had been 60 men killed and wounded,—that of the enemy was afterwards ascertained to be nearly 100; but their strong place had been forced in their teeth, the *purdah* (curtain) of their country had been lifted, and they had been well thrashed in fair fight. We had only one European officer wounded, Major Coke, who received a ball through the shoulder, but did not quit the field till the end of the action. The camp remained at Hurrunbole for three days, during which strong parties were daily despatched in different directions, to burn the enemy's villages, destroy his crops, and do as much damage as possible—a barbarous system of warfare, but the only effectual means of bringing these robber tribes to their senses. Their cattle had all been driven to the interior, and we did not get a single head of any kind.

Having sent back our wounded, and received fresh supplies, we again moved on up the principal pass, the road getting worse and worse as we advanced. No resistance was offered, and again our parties ravaged the surrounding country, their track marked by the smoke of the burning villages. All the mosques, however, were scrupulously spared, and trees were not cut down. I went out every day, with one party or another, to survey this unknown region, and managed to make a tolerable map before we left the hills. Bhartee, the so-called capital, was a miserable little village, but standing in a beautiful patch of cultivation, now covered with green wheat, and agreeably diversified with clumps of trees; the whole forming a lovely little oasis amongst the surrounding barren country.

At length we had penetrated thirty miles into the hills, and had arrived close to the foot of the Kala Roh, or high range. Beyond this it would have been impossible to drag the heavy guns with horses; but five elephants, which had been sent for, had arrived, and Captain Sladen made arrangements for carrying his guns on these animals, the huge beasts walking off with a 9-pounder on their backs without much trouble.

But the Bozdars were by this time thoroughly disheartened; they saw we were prepared to follow them up till they gave in. Day after day their green crops were being destroyed, and we had called in the Oosterances, a small but warlike tribe, who were at feud with them, to come down on their flank, and share in the plunder of their country.

So one morning the Bozdar chiefs mounted their horses, and rode into our camp suing for peace, and saying they were at our mercy. They were civilly received, and at a solemn Durbar the terms of treaty were settled by the Civil Officer and the Brigadier acting in concert.

For every man they had slain in their forays, 125 rupees were to be paid; and 50 rupees for every wounded man,—this being the regular price of blood in the hills.

All property plundered within the last year was to be restored or replaced. They engaged to give hostages for good behaviour in future, by two of their chiefs residing under surveillance at Dera Ghazee Khan; finally, 300 sheep were to be delivered as an *earnest* gift for the use of the troops.

It was a curious sight to see these wild Belooch chiefs, in their flowing robes and long hair halfway down their backs, seated in a circle in front of a few white men, while our own dark-faced soldiers stood around listening to the discussion. The chiefs accepted our terms, which were probably milder than they expected; they honourably fulfilled their engagements, and have never since given the smallest trouble. A few months afterwads they furnished a contingent for the defence of the frontier, when troops had been withdrawn to aid in the suppression of the mutiny in Hindustan.

Thus terminated this interesting little campaign, one of the most difficult and successful of the many frontier fights. Part of our force returned by the same road by which we had advanced. Part went round by another route, to give us a good look at the country, and to enable me to complete my survey.

On the 26th, we were again assembled at Towsa, having been nearly three weeks in the hills. The Brigadier issued a farewell order to officers and men, thanking them for their exertions, and the officers entertained him at dinner that night, and drank his health with loud cheers. The following day the force was broken up; the troops marched for their several destinations, and I rode back to Dera Ghazee Khan. Little did any of us think that our next place of meeting would be Delhi.

CHAPTER II.

THE MUTINIES.

In May, 1857, the rumours which had been afloat for the last three months as to the mutinous disposition of a portion of the Bengal Army, with respect to the question of the greased cartridges, were fearfully and unexpectedly confirmed by the news of the massacres of Meerut and Delhi, which suddenly startled our ears. After my return from the Bozdar Expedition, I had remained in my district quietly employed in ordinary engineering duties, and marching about as usual, until the commencement of the hot weather necessitated a return to Dera Ghazee Khan.

The regiments then stationed there were the 1st Seikh Infantry, the 2nd Punjab Infantry, and the 3rd Punjab Cavalry. About six weeks had elapsed since our return from the above expedition, and officers and men were living quietly in cantonments, having made themselves comfortable for the hot weather, little dreaming of the very different sort of hot weather they were most of them to pass through.

The news first reached me in a private letter, and was naturally not credited; but the newspapers from Lahore, bringing the intelligence of the disarming of the Native regiments at Mean-meer, soon placed the question beyond doubt.

No particular fears were, however, entertained by us in the matter. The idea of a general rising, even among the Poorbeah Army, was at that time looked upon as absurd, and the frontier officers at any rate looked with confidence to their splendid regiments, who had fought under them incessantly against men of their own colour and faith during the last eight years.

The mutiny, however, spread like wildfire, even in the Punjab, but it was met with characteristic energy by the Local Government. Immediately on the great news being known at Peshawur, a council of war was held, at which Brigadiers Cotton and Neville Chamberlain, Colonels Edwardes and Nicholson were present, and a moveable column formed, whose objects were declared to be to put down open mutiny by force wherever it existed. An energy was displayed by all classes throughout the "Model Province," which paralyzed the mutineers, and gave confidence to the well-affected. The fortresses and magazines of Ferozepore, Phillour, and Govindghur were at once occupied by Europeans. But at Moultan, whose fort contained one-third of the whole ammunition of the Punjab, there were only sixty British soldiers, while two regular Native regiments, a Native Police battalion, principally composed of Hindustanees, a Native troop of Horse Artillery, and the 1st Irregular Cavalry, consisting, like other similar regiments, almost entirely of Hindustanee Sowars, showed how little was the idea of danger from our Native troops dreamed of at the head-quarters of the army.

Sir John Lawrence at once saw the danger. Had the Moultan fort been seized by the rebels, with its stores and munitions of war, the whole of the west of the Punjab would probably have gone, and the tranquillity of the province been permanently destroyed. There was not a European soldier nearer than Lahore, 200 miles distant. It was therefore resolved at once to employ the frontier troops to act against the mutinous regular army. An express was despatched from Rawul Pindee, where the Chief Commissioner then was, down the line of border posts to the officers at Dera Ghazee Khan and Asnee. But the orders issued had already been acted upon by those officers on their own responsibility. A mutinous spirit had already appeared in the Moultan regiments; and about the 16th of May news was received that the presence of a portion of the frontier troops was earnestly desired. Within two hours of the message being received, the 2nd Regiment of Punjab Infantry was marching out of the station: their commanding officer told them, in a few spirited words, that the regular army had been faithless to their salt, and that the Government had called on *them* to act against their mutinous brethren. The address was received with a wild Pathan yell that told how cordial was the hatred of the Poorbeah by the Punjabee. The 1st Punjab Cavalry was at the same time marched up from Asnee, and crossed over to Moultan, and the presence of these two regiments at that station enabled the Commandant, Major Crawford Chamberlain, shortly afterwards to disarm the 62nd and 69th Native Infantry without bloodshed, and unassisted by any Europeans but sixty Artillerymen.

To supply the place of the absent corps, the defence of the frontier was partially entrusted to hastily raised levies. The Belooch is a man of war from his youth up. The old feudal institutions of the tribes had been carefully maintained by the British Government; and when the Deputy Commissioner of the district called upon the several chiefs for their contingents, the call was promptly and faithfully responded to.

The same measures were pursued in the other frontier stations with equal success; so that Government was enabled to withdraw the 1st Punjab

Cavalry, wings of the 2nd and 5th Punjab Cavalry, and the 1st, 2nd, and 4th Punjab Infantry, to reinforce the army before Delhi, without jeopardizing the peace of the frontier.

To the end of the struggle the firmness and tact of the Punjab officers prevented an explosion, which might have brought down 100,000 armed and warlike Mussulman fanatics to give ample employment to the whole resources of the Local Government.

Things passed quietly on at Dera Ghazee Khan after this, until the mutinous infection seized the Poorbeahs of the 3rd Punjab Cavalry at this station, and we heard with uneasiness of secret meetings in the lines at night, and felt that a very little might precipitate an outbreak. The Punjabees of the corps were, however, known to be staunch, and gave all the information in their power to the commanding officer; we felt we could rely on the Seikh Infantry; and as the cavalry lines were a mile away from the rest of the station, we felt it extremely unlikely that any violent outbreak would occur, or that they would attempt anything more than escaping with their horses and arms to Delhi.

Two guns were also sent down at this time from the battery at Dera Ismail Khan; and the Commandant of the cavalry taking measures to rid himself quietly of the bad characters, by discharging them, or keeping them away from head-quarters on outpost duty, the bad feeling in the regiment disappeared, and no explosion ever took place, the regiment subsequently doing excellent service on the frontier.

All this time we waited with impatience day after day for the news of the capture of Delhi, feeling that this would at once check the mutinous spirit of the army, and never doubting but that in a week or two the place must fall. Under this idea, I wrote to the Secretary to the Chief Commissioner, to remind him that I had a company of Punjab Sappers and Miners under me, and proposing that I should be allowed to take them down to join the Irregular Army then being raised by General Van Cortlandt, for service in the Hansee and Hissar districts. Knowing that the General had no Sappers and no Engineer officer with him, I thought my services might probably be most useful in that direction.

In reply to my application, I was directed to send off the Sapper Company, but was informed that my own services could not be spared from the frontier. Shortly afterwards I again wrote, proposing to raise some companies of Punjabee Sappers of different castes, hoping to be allowed to take them down to Delhi. This, however, was again refused, doubtless for good and sufficient reasons, and I gave up all idea of being actively employed.

So passed June and July: from time to time we heard the news of the successive outbreaks of the Sepoys at the stations in the Punjab, which resulted generally in their defeat, and sometimes their extermination, as they attempted to make for Delhi.

The moveable column, under the energetic guidance of Brigadier-General Nicholson, destroyed the 55th at Murdan, and the 46th at Trimmoo Ghat; the 4th and 33rd were disarmed, the 10th Irregular Cavalry dismounted and disbanded. No mutineers met with the slightest mercy; and the stern character of the General, well known throughout the Punjab, the rapidity of his marches at the hottest time of the year, and the immediate execution of every man taken in arms, struck terror into all evil-doers, and released Government from all fear of the Sepoy rebels. Confident in his own strength and the loyalty of the mass of the population, Sir John Lawrence, who had already despatched large succours to the Delhi army, resolved to send General Nicholson and his column thither also.

From Hindustan we heard of the defection of regiment after regiment, and the loss of district after district; of massacres of our countrymen and countrywomen; of ladies and children flying to the hill stations for refuge; and of the desperate and heroic efforts everywhere made by the small scattered bands of Englishmen to restrain the fearful torrent. Our Delhi news told us of the advance of our troops from Meerut and Delhi; of the battles of the Hindun and Badlee-Ka-Serai; of the deaths of the Commander-in-Chief, General Barnard, and the Adjutant-General of the army; of the series of desperate attacks made on our position by the tenfold force of the mutineers, and their invariable bloody repulse, though often at a heavy loss of valuable lives. It was only by slow degrees that we learned that our force was, in truth, the besieged party, and that but for the great natural strength of the position we had taken up, even the desperate valour of our troops, who felt that on the retaining of our position depended the fate of the empire, would hardly have enabled us to hold our own so long. The severity of the heat, and the harassing nature of the duties, had already told fearfully on the men, and the continual reinforcements from the Punjab at first barely supplied the drain caused by sickness and casualties. Twice was it resolved to terminate the suspense, by an attempt to carry the city by a *coup de main;* but the fearful consequences of failure, and the desperate risk of the attempt, caused the Generals in command to counter-order the assault at the last moment; and no one can now deny that they were right in so doing.

Beyond Delhi our news was a blank. The whole country was in the enemy's hands, and our only means of communication was round by Bombay and Calcutta, where the ignorance of what was passing between Allahabad and Delhi was almost as great as our own. To give some idea of this ignorance, I may mention that it was generally rumoured in camp that Sir Hugh Wheeler, with six European regiments, was advancing from below to reinforce the army at Delhi, nearly a month after he and his weak detachment had been massacred at Cawnpore.

That was, indeed, a fearful time of anxiety, and none who passed through it can ever forget it.

CHAPTER III.

FROM DERA GHAZEE KHAN TO DELHI.

On the 25th of July I received an official letter, informing me that my services had been applied for by the Chief Engineer of the Delhi Field Force, and I was ordered to make over charge of my civil and military work to an officer at the station, and to proceed with all possible despatch, at the public expense, to join the camp.

On the evening of the 26th, I left the station on horseback for a moonlight ride to Moultan, forty-five miles distant.

But the end of July is not a favourable time for travelling in that part of the world, where the rivers, swollen to their highest, inundate the whole country around, and render the district roads all but impassable.

I was four hours crossing the Indus; and after a ride of twenty-six miles through mud and water, found myself only at Mozuffergurh, at nine o'clock in the morning. Being only just off a sick bed, I thought it advisable to wait during the heat of the day; and another night's ride, and a very tedious passage over the Chenab, brought me safely to Moultan.

Here I was most hospitably received by De B——, of the artillery, who sighed that he was not going down with me. The following evening found me seated on the mail cart, *en route* to Lahore. The Indian reader will understand the pleasures of a long journey in the mail cart, over a Kucha road in the month of July: to the English reader it may be necessary to explain that the said vehicle is on two wheels, and drawn by two horses, who, after obstinately refusing to stir a step at starting, generally dash off at the rate of 12 miles an hour, when they do move, and continue that pace until they arrive at the end of the stage, about six miles distant. The bumping and jolting endured by the unhappy passenger, over a road guiltless of metalling, and full of holes and ruts, are not improving to the bones or temper; but you get over your ground at a great pace (for India), and anything is preferable to the three miles an hour and eternal jog-jogging of a palanquin.

At ten a.m. the following day I had accomplished 130 miles of my 210; but go on as I had intended I could not, and I stopped for the day at the little civil station of Googaira, afterwards the scene of the only outbreak of any portion of the population that occurred in the Punjab. The same evening I left by another mail cart, and early on the following morning, the 31st of July, arrived at the Lahore Dák Bungalow. This building was full of officers on their way to Delhi, and many were the greetings between friends who never expected to meet in this place on such an errand.

In Anarkullee (the old cantonment) new police levies, and the recruits for the new Punjab regiments, were being incessantly enrolled and drilled; and I recognized the tall burly form of the Chief Commissioner, inspecting a body of newly raised aspirants for martial glory, who looked particularly stiff and solemn under the awful inspection to which they were being subjected. The whole station, however, was in a ferment, owing to a more exciting cause. The 26th N.I., which, with the 16th, 49th, and 8th Light Cavalry, had been disarmed on the 13th May, had broken out only the previous day, murdered their commanding officer, Major Spencer, a worthy, kind man, who had served twenty-five years with them, and had fled in a body towards the hills. At first, it was naturally supposed they had taken the Delhi road, and probably their first day's march was only a blind; however that may be, the military authorities were thrown off the scent.

But a hue-and-cry was raised all over the country against them: the population turned upon them; Mr. Cooper, the Deputy Commissioner of the Umritsir district, pursued them with a body of police, and in two days from the date of their atrocious murder the regiment was all but exterminated.

It was said to have been a concerted plot with men of the other disarmed regiments, that one of them should thus run to entice the Europeans to follow them, when the rest should rise and murder the women and children in the cantonments; but from many proofs, it was evident that whatever plot might have been hatched between some of the scoundrels, a great part of the regiment fled from the fear of being cut up by the Europeans, when they heard of the murder of their commanding officer. In fact, this was only another instance of what an intelligent native officer (a Poorbeah Brahmin) said to me as to the cause of the mutinies; "Sir, there is one knave and nine fools; the knave compromises the others, and then tells them it is too late to draw back; they either actively join, or run away for fear of the Europeans' vengeance." I asked this man, at the same time, if the greased cartridges really were the cause of the revolt among the Sepoys themselves—adding, that we believed the cartridge question was simply put forward as a pretext. He said, "Of course he did not know who had first originated the grievance, but that, and that alone, was the exciting cause amongst the Sepoys;" he said, too, that a story was very prevalent amongst the bazaars that Government had caused human bones to be ground up with the ottah served out to the men to make their bread with, in order to deprive them of their caste. "I remember," he continued, "precisely a similar panic some years ago, when it was reported that the European doctors caught native children, and hung them up by their heels over a fire to distil mummiai (a sort of fabulous unguent) from them; the panic was so great that, as my regiment passed through village after village on the line of march, not a child was to be seen, their mothers having carefully concealed them."

At the Lahore Dâk Bungalow I met Colonel F——, lately in command of the 46th N.I. When that regiment mutinied at Sealkote, together with the 9th Light Cavalry, the Colonel was hidden by his Sepoys all day long in a barrack; they refused to let him go out, alleging that the cavalry would kill him, as indeed they did many officers on that day, but brought him cheroots and brandy and water from the mess, and urged him to join the rebel cause, promising him 2,000 rupees a month, and leave to the hills every hot season! In the evening they conveyed him in safety to the fort, whither the rest of the Europeans had fled.

On the following day I drove out to the new Lahore cantonments at Mean-Meer, four miles from Anarkullee, which I had helped to build some five years before. The European artillery and H.M.'s 81st Regiment were all under arms, watching the three remaining disarmed regiments. Nearly all the station bungalows were deserted; the ladies and children being either in the fort or in one or two of the soldiers' barracks, which had been made over for their accommodation. A strong picket of European artillery and new Seikh levies was maintained at the church to protect the building, the finest in Upper India, and the whole of this large cantonment wore the same martial yet deserted appearance. Things remained in this state for some time afterwards, until at length the disarmed Sepoys were ejected from their lines, which were all pulled down; the men encamped in the open, with standing pickets around them, and within easy range of the artillery guns.

A return of my old enemy, fever and ague, detained me two more days at Lahore, and I was recommended not to go on to Delhi, where a sick man would not have been of much use. Feeling pretty sure, however, that the excitement and change of scene would do more for me than medicine, I started on the evening of the 1st of August for Umritsir, in company with a brother officer, Lieut. H——, who had just come down from Peshawur, and was bound for Delhi, like myself.

The road, as far as the river Beas, being metalled, we proceeded along very comfortably for about forty miles in a palkee gharee, and then were obliged to change to the abominable mail cart, which jolted us in fine style to Jullundur, at about 2 p.m., when it instantly commenced to pour with rain, and we had to wait some hours before we judged it advisable to proceed on our journey. While seated in the Jullundur Dák Bungalow, we were startled by a smart shock of an earthquake, which made the house rock and creak, and us to jump up like a shot. This fine station was almost deserted, the European regiment lately occupying it being at Delhi, and the Native corps having previously mutinied and marched off in a body to the same place, but on the wrong side. A vigorous pursuit might have overtaken them as they reached the Sutlej; and the General Officer in command was greatly blamed that the pursuing Europeans and artillery did not destroy them, in forcing the passage of that river, where Mr. Ricketts, the Deputy Commissioner of Loodiana, with one gun and three companies of a Seikh Corps, bravely disputed their crossing for several hours, trusting that the pursuing columns would be close on their heels.

The only troops now occupying the station were some of the Jheend Rajah's auxiliaries, and one of Sir J. Lawrence's newly raised Punjab regiments.

In the evening we proceeded onwards on our journey, passed the strong little fort of Phillour, whose magazine supplied the siege train for Delhi, and after a tedious passage over the Sutlej by moonlight, arrived at Loodiana early in the morning.

The tents of some more of our friendly allies were here pitched, but being anxious to get on as the weather was rainy, we did not stop to breakfast until we had accomplished another forty miles along the well-metalled Umballa road, when we pulled up for an hour at the Kana-Ke-Serai Bungalow, and again pushed on for Umballa.

Fifteen miles further we overtook General Nicholson's column, which was in full march for Delhi. It consisted of H.M.'s 52nd Light Infantry, 2nd Punjab Infantry, a wing of a Punjab Police Battalion, and 200 Moultanee Horse, with Bouchier's Light Field Battery,—a small force, but whose avenging march, under their stern leader, had been like the track of the destroying angel through the land.

As we stopped to change horses, the General sent out to us to take one of his officers on to Umballa; and as my companion knew him, I went with him to the tent, and, for the first time, met this remarkable man. Imagine a man 6 feet 2 inches high, and powerfully made in proportion, with a massive-looking head and face, short, curly grey hair, and long black beard—the expression stern and quick, according well with the deep voice and abrupt speech, but full of animation, and with a very pleasant smile.

The whole face and figure showed a man of iron constitution, indomitable energy and resolution, great self-reliance, and born to command; and I could quite understand the extraordinary influence he possessed over all who came in contact with him, in spite of a *hauteur* of manner and a certain want of tact, which often gave offence to men who did not know the sterling qualities of his character.

In the evening we arrived at Umballa, and repaired to the hotel, which, however, was so full of sick and wounded officers coming from the camp, and sound officers going there, that we had to put up at the Dák Bungalow, and only dine and breakfast at the table d'hôte.

Of course, we eagerly asked questions of the state and prospects of the siege, which had now been two months nominally going on, and as we found there was no immediate prospect of an assault, as had been rumoured at Lahore, we stayed at Umballa a couple of days to make purchases, and send on our traps by the army transport train. We were still 110 miles from Delhi, but this was the last station on the road where we could provide ourselves with camp requisites.

General Nicholson's force marched into Umballa the following day; and General Wilson having telegraphed to him to come on alone to consult about future proceedings, he left us at the Dák Bungalow, and went on to Delhi by the mail cart.

Umballa looked rather more lively than the other stations we had passed through, as its situation naturally made it a sort of depôt for all stores and troops going down to the army. Large convoys were daily leaving for the camp, and the regular din of war seened first to strike on one's ear here. Most of these convoys could only be escorted by a few raw levies; we could spare no other troops, and the infatuation that led the rebels to permit us to keep open this great line of communication with the Punjab, with scarcely an attempt on their part at interruption, can only be regarded as one of the many instances of providential interference in our favour.

On the evening of the 6th August we again mounted the mail cart, and by the morning had reached Kurnaul, once a large and favourite cantonment, but afterwards abandoned on the score of its insalubrity. Here we breakfasted, and then went on to Lussowlie, thirty miles only from Delhi, where we found a strong body of the Jheend Rajah's troops keeping open our communication.

On once more to Bhyee, where we found another body of raw levies, and then to Aleepore, only eight miles from the camp, where a strong picket of our own Punjab cavalry showed we had at length reached the outskirts of the army. Here I had the pleasure of meeting two old Derajat friends, in the officers of the picket, who were rather astonished to see me here, our last parting having been in the Bozdar Hills, with as little idea of meeting at Delhi as at Damascus.

Here, too, we first heard the sullen boom of the guns from the camp; and, unaware that this went on incessantly, we became doubly anxious to push on, thinking a regular fight was coming off.

Changing horses for the last time, and escorted by two Sowars (as our cart carried the mails), we drove at length into camp, and jumped down at the Post Office tent, close to where the General's flag was flying.

I had accomplished my journey of 600 miles without any hindrance, or even misadventure, and think, if some of the gentlemen who talked so glibly at home of a popular rebellion had accompanied me, they could not have had a stronger contradiction to their opinions. I meditated on this fact; it seemed to me a striking one, and I did not altogether "despair of the Republic."

CHAPTER IV.

THE BRITISH POSITION BEFORE DELHI.

PUSHING our way amongst swarms of camp followers, and guided by a man lent to us by the postmaster, we quickly reached the Engineers' Camp, and found some old and familiar and some new faces amongst the officers assembled at the mess.

A house that had escaped the general wreck gave us a good sized room for our mess, and for sitting in during the heat of the day. The tents were pitched in the ground adjoining, and beyond the tents was the Engineer park. It was nearly dinner-time when we arrived, and being, besides, very tired, I was quite content to wait till the following morning to have a look at the position.

At sunrise, I rode up to the flag-staff tower on the ridge, and thence had an excellent view of our camp, the city, and the adjoining ground, which had been, and was still to be, the scene of so much desperate fighting.

This position I will now attempt to describe.

The city of Delhi lies on the right bank of the

Jumna, 120 miles above the other Mogul capital, Agra, which is also on the right bank. The river washes the east face of the city, forming the chord of an arc, of which the rest of the city wall is the perimeter.

The length from north to south is about two miles; the extreme breadth from east to west, about three miles; the area enclosed within the walls probably four square miles.

The place is entirely surrounded by the aforesaid walls, which consist of long curtains, with bastions at different intervals, the whole defended by a ditch and a good glacis. The walls are built of stone and lime, and had always been kept in thorough repair.

The bastions were of modern construction, and capable of mounting twelve to eighteen guns each. There was, however, only a musketry parapet along the connecting walls, there being no terre-plein behind the curtains for guns.

On the river side was the King's palace, a native fort of considerable size, with high walls of red sandstone, flanked by round towers, and defended by a ditch. Close to the palace, and connected with it by a bridge over an arm of the river, was the Selimgurh, an old native fort, opposite to which, and under the fire of its guns, was the bridge of boats leading to the Meerut road, on the other side of the river.

The breadth of the Jumna at Delhi is about 1,000 yards; it is very winding and shallow, with numerous sand-banks, the deep channel being very narrow. A low ridge of sandstone runs from the river obliquely towards the north face of the city, and, at the nearest point, is distant from it about 1,200 yards. This ridge terminates abruptly at the Subzee-Mundee suburb, after extending for a length of 2,000 yards, but is immediately after resumed, and then stretches away in a south-westerly direction.

The East Jumna Canal, and the Grand Trunk Road to the Punjab, both take advantage of this break in the ridge to run into the city.

Between this ridge and the city walls the ground is stony, very broken and undulating, and covered with trees and grass. On the west side the ground is more open from the city to the large suburbs of Kissengung and Paharipore, which join on to the Subzee-Mundee.

On the south side the ground is covered for miles with the ruins of temples, palaces, and tombs, the relics of old Delhi.

The cantonments were on the north side of the ridge. The civil lines on the opposite side, extending irregularly towards the city.

The Church, the *Delhi Gazette* Press, the Delhi Bank, and many other buildings belonging to

Europeans, were all inside the walls at the north end of the city. The magazine was also there, consisting of a great mass of buildings inside a square inclosure, containing 200 guns of heavy calibre, and an almost inexhaustible supply of ammunition.

From the centre of the town rose the Jumma Musjid, one of the noblest specimens of Moslem architecture in the world. Built of great blocks of red sandstone, with three domes of white marble, and raised upon a terrace fifty feet in height, it towered high above the city, and was visible at a great distance.

The population of modern Delhi by the last census was about 150,000 souls.

The British camp was pitched in and around cantonments on the north side of the ridge which formed the great strength of our position. The river well protected our left flank, but our right only rested on the Subzee-Mundee, which thus was the key of our position, as by it alone could our flank be turned and our communications with the Punjab threatened, unless by making a wide sweep of many miles in extent. The enemy knew this as well as we did, and many a desperate contest had already taken place in the houses and streets of that suburb; but gradually we had cleared away the cover, and strengthened this important post, until the attacks on it became fainter and fainter.

In front of the Subzee-Mundee post was the Sammy House, a small temple, which formed our most advanced picket, and was also the scene of many a tough fight. The Engineers had connected it with the Subzee-Mundee by a line of breast-works, including the crow's nest, a high, craggy mass of rock, which was a favourite post for our riflemen.

On the extreme right point of the ridge itself was our heavy gun battery, known as the Right Battery; it was 1,200 yards from the city wall, and its duties were to pound the Moree Bastion at the north-west corner of the city whenever it opened fire, and to reply to the enfilading batteries which the enemy had established in Paharipore.

Moving now along the ridge to our left, we come to the heavy mortar battery, sunk in a hollow on the slope; and again, going on, we reach Hindoo Rao's house, a large upper storied building with out-offices, which formed the main picket. In front of it was the centre half-moon battery.

Three hundred yards further to the left, and we come to the Observatory, close to which our left heavy gun battery was erected. The ground immediately behind this position, at the bottom of the slope, was known as the Valley of Death, a short cut to camp lying through it, which was much oftener avoided than traversed.

Left of the Observatory was the next picket, the Mosque; and beyond this again, the Flagstaff Tower, a favourite resort of officers when off duty, from which a fine view could be obtained of the whole position.

Now we leave the high ground, as the ridge runs back from this point, and, still going left, we come to Metcalfe House, on the river, in the stables and cow-house of which our most advanced pickets on this side were established.

One road, to the Cashmere Gate of the city, led from cantonments past Metcalfe's Park; another road, to the Lahore Gate, turned off the ridge close to the Observatory.

With the help of the plan, the reader will, perhaps, be able to comprehend this explanation, which I have endeavoured not to make too complicated by detailing the minor breast-works, light gun batteries, &c., which had been at different times thrown up to strengthen our position.

He will have understood by this account that we were rather besieged than besieging, our numbers being much too weak to attempt an assault, and our great aim being to hold our strong position against attack with the smallest possible expenditure of men, that when our reinforcements and siege guns should arrive, we might descend from our heights, and assault with success. Of course, an investment of the city was out of the question: it was seven miles round, not including the river face, which would also have required a body of men to watch it from the bridge of boats. We were opposite the north face, and must remain there, as we thus covered our line of communication, the Umballa road, by which all supplies and reinforcements reached us.

The British force before Delhi, at this period, consisted of the following troops:—

Artillery.—Tomb's, Turner's, Kennington's, and Money's troops of Horse Artillery; Scott's Light Field Battery, and a few heavy guns; the only 24-pounders being those taken from the enemy in action.

Engineers.—About two companies of Bengal Sappers; six companies of the Punjab Sappers; and about 800 new Pioneers.

Cavalry.—H.M.'s 9th Lancers; one squadron of the 6th Carabineers; one squadron from each of the following regiments:— 1st, 2nd, and 5th Punjab Cavalry; Guide Cavalry; Hodson's Horse.

Infantry.—H.M.'s 60th Rifles; H.M.'s 75th; one wing of the 61st; one wing of the 8th; the Hon. Company's 1st and 2nd Bengal Fusileers; 1st Punjab Infantry; Guide Corps; 4th Seikh Infantry;

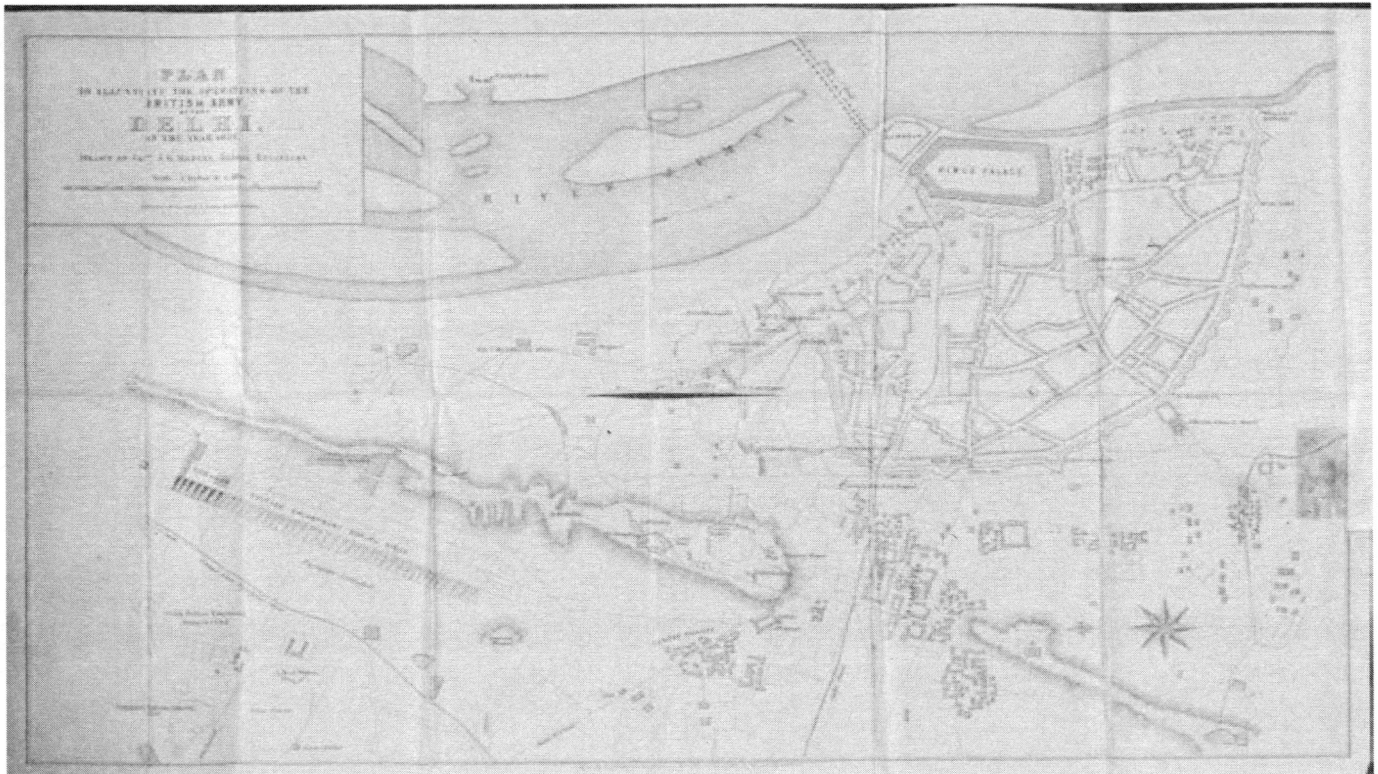
PLAN
BRITISH ARMY
DELHI.
KINGS PALACE

Nusseree Battalion, and Kumaon Battalion (both Goorkhas).

All the above regiments were very weak: constant fighting, sickness, and exposure having already done their work; and the whole force, at this period, did not number more than 6,000 men.

The day after my arrival I went to pay my respects to General Wilson, commanding the army, and found a tall, soldier-like man, with whose personal appearance the public is, probably, well acquainted by this time. In the evening I went out with T——, our able second in command of the Engineers, to have a look at our batteries. We drove up to the Observatory in a dog-cart, but the Moree Bastion was sending a few shot in our direction, and the horse plunged so with fright that he nearly ran away with us. Dismounting, we entered the left battery, which was then replying to the fire of the Moree, and had not been there five minutes, when a well-aimed shell from that bastion, bursting (luckily, rather short), sent a shower of stones and dust about us, and gave one of the Artillery officers a sharp cut on the skull. We then went on, and looked at the several batteries I have already described, meeting with no other adventure. The usual desultory firing was going on from the Moree and from Paharipore, and as we descended the slope of the ridge and approached the Sammy House, the continual ping-ping of musket bullets over our heads showed we were within range of the enemy's skirmishers in the dense brushwood and copses of trees around. This sort of annoyance was perpetual, and never entirely ceased by night or day. Pandy * had plenty of men, and could afford to throw away plenty of ammunition on the speculation of a chance shot now and then knocking over a man, which, of course, it did. We used often to see his men coming out from the city to relieve his various pickets at Ludlow Castle, &c., though we had not then a clear relief for all our pickets, in fact two-thirds of the infantry were constantly on duty at one time; and the artillery were for days and days together without any relief at all. It may be imagined how harassing this duty was to our jaded troops. The heat of the sun was, of course, excessive at this time of the year; rain fell constantly, and the country all round was a swamp, while the swarms of flies and musquitoes, and the horrible stench of dead animals and dead men, made every picket and position held by the troops a little purgatory.

* This term, Pandy, now so well known as the *nom de guerre* by which we dubbed the rebels throughout the campaign, was derived from the circumstance of the first rebel (executed at Barrackpore) bearing the name of Mungul Pandy. Our Punjabee and Goorkha soldiers christened the rebels *Mattadeen*, a common Hindoo name.

When Pandy fancied we were off our guard, or weakened, by having to send off detachments to bring in stores, &c., or when, for any other reason, he had screwed up his courage sufficiently, he would make a general attack on our position. At first, in June and July, these were very serious affairs; light and heavy guns were brought out, and swarms of skirmishers, throwing themselves into the dense cover and broken ground around, would assail the whole front and the right flank, and more than once pressed our rear severely. Then our men would make a sortie from our position at different points, and after several hours of hard fighting Pandy would be driven back, and pursued up to the walls, with the loss, probably, of some of his guns, and many hundreds of killed and wounded, and our weary troops would get a temporary repose, perhaps to be attacked the next day in a similar manner. Nor were our losses by any means slight on these occasions, especially considering the small number of the besieging force. But matters were now much altered for the better; our position was greatly strengthened, our numbers increased, and Pandy, beaten so often, had lost much of his pluck. He now attacked us from greater distances. Our men were kept well under cover, and the attacks repulsed with very trifling casualties.

CHAPTER V.

DELHI IN AUGUST, 1857.

Two or three days after my arrival, I had to take my first tour of duty at the Azadpore picket. This was the most unpleasant bit of work we had to do. The line of bridges over the Delhi Canal and Nujufghur Drain had all been blown up by us (except one), to prevent our flank being turned by the enemy crossing. The one saved was useful to our foraging parties, but was kept ready mined, with an Engineer officer always on duty, to blow it up in case of necessity. A cavalry picket was maintained at Azadpore, where the cantonment road turns off from the main line, and close to the aforesaid bridge. Here the Engineer on duty took up his residence for forty-eight hours, and accompanied the patrolling party of cavalry to see the state of the inundated country around, and to report on the depth of water in the canal. As this involved a ride of twelve miles through *slush* and water, and a return to a tent, where flies by day and musquitoes by night effectually prevented sleep, it was not a favourite duty. I went the usual round with the cavalry that day and the next, but nothing occurred worthy of note, and I returned to camp at the usual time, when relieved.

The present duties of the Engineers were at this time executed as follows:—

Under the Chief Engineer were the two Directing Engineers of the right and left. A Field Engineer went on duty every evening at 5 p.m., and was relieved every twenty-four hours. His head-quarters were at the Serai picket, in the Subzee-Mundee, and he had charge of all new work that was to be executed during the following night. An Assistant Field Engineer was stationed at Hindoo Rao's (the main picket), to do the ordinary repairs that were required at the different batteries. The working parties were sent down at dusk under their several officers, and worked away until dawn, when they were marched back to camp. As the reader probably knows, the principal part of the Engineers' work at a siege is invariably executed at night, for the two-fold object of secrecy and safety. At 1 p.m., when we were at tiffin, the order-book usually came round, and we all knew who were required during the next twenty-four hours. At four o'clock there was an early dinner for the officers on duty, who then went away with their respective working parties; some to make new breastworks; some to lay and construct fresh batteries, or to clear away the cover near the posts; to strengthen the posts themselves, or to cut brushwood, for making those useful auxiliaries to the Engineer—gabions and fascines.* All this time, too, the Engineer park was the scene of incessant activity, under its able director, Lieut. Brownlow. Siege materials were being collected in large quantities, and made, and stored up; the working parties of Sappers were practised at making field powder magazines, and laying platforms for the future siege batteries; experiments were carefully tried in the construction of different sorts of batteries, the loading and unloading of stores, the best methods of arranging workmen, of carrying materials, &c., &c., so that we might know perfectly what men and what time were required to execute certain work, and that no labour or time might be uselessly expended.

Our chief difficulty consisted in the want of trained Sappers. The head-quarters of the Bengal Sappers and Miners were at Roorkee when the mutiny broke out. They were at once ordered to

* I may take the liberty here of paying a just tribute to the excellent and orderly arrangements of our Brigade Major (Lieutenant Chesney), more particularly during the actual siege in September. Severe as the duty was, no officer was unnecessarily worked. An admirable routine was preserved, by which all knew when and where their presence would be required; and this not a little contributed to the rapid and complete success of the subsequent arduous operations.

Meerut, and marched there cheerfully enough, when an attempt to take away their regimental magazine from them made them break out in open revolt. They fled, were pursued, many cut down, and the rest dispersed to repair to Delhi, and give the enemy most valuable aid in his defence. Two or three companies, however, had been quietly disarmed in another part of the station; and on Brigadier Wilson's force leaving for Delhi, these men were rearmed, and accompanied that small column. They had behaved remarkably well ever since, and were the only trained Sappers we had, as they were the only remnant of the regular Native army that was now in camp. The numbers, however, sorely reduced by wounds and fatigue, were not more than 120 effective men when the siege really commenced.

Sir John Lawrence had raised and sent down to us several companies of Muzbees, or low caste Seikhs, who were eventually turned into pioneers, and were armed and partially disciplined. We had nearly 800 of these men.

Besides these, the Chief Engineer had enlisted a large body of common labourers on high pay, whose aid was invaluable from the first, in relieving the fighting men from the digging and trenching in such fearful weather. The utility of these men was so great, that they were gradually increased in number to 1,000, and though without arms and untrained, being, in fact, mere road coolies, rendered the most essential service during the siege, and, in spite of heavy casualties, worked cheerfully under fire.

Meanwhile, the Chief Engineer and his able second in command were employed in drawing up the project of the siege, as it was known that by the beginning of the following month the siege train, which would arrive from Phillour, and General Nicholson's column, which was on its march down, would so far swell our numbers as to give us a fair chance of success.

About ten days after my arrival in camp, I took my first turn of duty as Field Engineer of the day, And as it will serve to show the general nature of our work at this time, I will give an account of my twenty-four hours' spell.

At 5 p.m. I went down to the Subzee-Mundee Serai, and relieved the officer who had been on duty the previous twenty-four hours. The Directing Engineer then went with me to the Sammy House to show me the work he wanted to be executed during the night; and at dusk the working party ordered for this purpose came down, under a junior officer. A new breast-work had to be made, and, having traced it out before dark, the work was carried on through the night, and was pretty well completed before the morning. Having started this work, I went up to see after some repairs wanted in the right battery, where a small party of Sappers were employed. Then I paid a visit to a new mortar battery which had just been completed, and which was firing regularly every quarter of an hour throughout the night. The unfortunate officer and two men were alone awake from necessity, and the rest were comfortably snoring on the ground, perfectly undisturbed by the noise of the mortars. Every fifteen minutes the officer gave the word to "Light portfires!" and the men awoke, discharged the shell, proceeded to load again, and then laid down and went off to sleep, their turn being over till it came round again.

The usual amount of desultory firing was going on from the enemy—an occasional shot, or badly aimed shell, and a liberal sprinkling of musketry from the skirmishers in front. One soon got used to the ping-ing-ing of the bullets, though an occasional *thud*, as one struck the ground close to the feet, would make one start for a moment, and then walk on as before.

In the daytime there was no work to do, so I had a sleep, took a walk round the batteries to see if anything was wanted, and at five o'clock was in my turn relieved by the next man on duty.

Several of our officers were told off for reconnoitring and surveying, with the view of an accurate knowledge being obtained of the ground to our front. I was one amongst three or four others, and very exciting work it sometimes was. The first of these expeditions was, I remember, to determine the site of a new battery, to the left and in advance of the Sammy House, and which was to prevent our being annoyed by sorties from the Lahore Gate. Captain T—— and myself started early in the morning with an escort of four Goorkhas, and, getting into the long grass, we worked away in the proper direction, I surveying, and T—— looking out for squalls.

The Goorkhas looked upon it as fine fun, and made capital videttes; at last we found ourselves on the road leading to the Lahore Gate, our old friend the Moree Bastion, with which we had so often exchanged civilities, looking us straight in the face. Several of the enemy's Sepoys were coming jauntily down the road, when suddenly they saw us, not 200 yards off, and were brought up all standing with surprise. T—— then levelled his telescope at them, on which they took to their heels, and sang out to their friends in the Moree, and the next moment a bright flash and the whish-sh of a round shot over our heads warned us to beat a retreat, which we did very composedly.

The battery, whose site was chosen on this expedition, was shortly afterwards constructed as a preliminary operation to the attack, which was to take place when the siege train should arrive. It was on an isolated plateau, 900 yards from the Moree Bastion, and being much nearer to the enemy than any of the old batteries, was not finished without several casualties. It was made for six light guns, and was connected by a trench with the Sammy House on the right. W——, of our corps, lost his left arm here, by an unlucky shell from the Moree, which smashed the limb to pieces, and knocked over two Sappers. He had just been relieved from his turn of duty, and was about to return to camp, waiting for a minute to explain the line of fire for the embrasures to his successor, when the unfortunate shot struck him, and deprived us of the services of a valuable officer for the rest of the siege.

Somewhat later in the month we had another reconnoitring party on a larger scale, to survey a nullah, which was to be turned into our first parallel eventually.

This time we went with a guard of, I think, sixty Goorkhas. We crept down into the nullah, and, dividing the work amongst us, commenced surveying and plotting away at a great pace, our movements being considerably accelerated by the knowledge that we were 700 yards from our own line of pickets, and that the ground was not very favourable for running. We had very nearly completed our work, and would very likely have got off unobserved, when some Pandy grass-cutters spied us out, and ran off to the Cashmere Gate. The enemy sallied out in great force, and commenced to fire from a long distance, until they had thoroughly ascertained how small our party was, when they got more bold, and, sneaking through the long grass in swarms, tried to get round and cut us off, keeping up a teazing fire. The Goorkhas were ordered not to fire, and fell back very steadily, while we went on surveying, resolved to finish our work, in spite of all the Pandies in creation. I was comfortably seated under a small tree which formed a sort of protection, and was busy taking angles, when a puff of smoke rose from the Cashmere Bastion, and a shower of grape came just over us, tearing the tree to pieces all around. This was rather too close to be pleasant, and a second shot immediately afterwards, which threw the dust and stones right over us as it ploughed up the ground, made us execute a rapid "flank" movement, which took us out of range of the gun. We had done our work, and walked quietly towards Hindoo Rao's, but Pandy knew he should get a chance as we went up the slope of the hill, and let drive with a round shot by way of a parting hint. Their skirmishers followed us up pretty close, when the Goorkhas prayed to be allowed to have just one shot before the fun was over, and, on receiving permission from Captain T——, threw themselves into the grass, and commenced a file firing, which caused Pandy to beat a precipitate retreat, and it was with some difficulty we prevented the Goorkhas from following them up. As we were nearly home, I asked the little native officer who was with us, if any of his men were hit. "Oh, yes," he said, "one was hit." "Where was he?" "Oh, he was coming along all right." And so he was, too, with a little help, yet the man was shot through the groin, and died the same night; another man was hit in the thigh, but not badly; these were our only two casualties. On arriving at Hindoo Rao's, we found General Wilson and some of his staff, who had been watching our proceedings rather anxiously.

Shortly before this occurred, the camp was enlivened by a sharp fight which took place on the 12th of August. Pandy had been keeping up an annoying sort of skirmishing with our advanced picket on the left of Metcalfe's Stable for many days, and had at length brought out some light guns into the open, with which he made this post a very uncom fortable one for us, knocking over many of our men. It was, therefore, determined to capture these guns; and Brigadier Showers, with H.M.'s 75th, the

1st Fusileers, Coke's Punjab Rifles, and some guns and cavalry, sallied down the road at day-dawn on the 12th, and, after a sharp fight, brought in the four guns in triumph, killing a good number of the enemy. Two of our officers accompanied the party, but as I was not there myself, I can give no detailed account of the fight.

A considerable annoyance was caused on the left of our camp by a heavy gun battery, which the enemy had constructed on the other side of the river, immediately opposite our camp. As the bridge of boats was entirely in their possession, we had no immediate means of crossing to attack the battery, and were obliged to grin and bear it. The distance was nearly 2,000 yards, and the shooting not very good, but Coke's regiment, which held the ground on the extreme left, shifted its camp a little so as to be protected from this fire. On the 14th, Nicholson's column marched into camp, bringing us a welcome reinforcement of about 2,000 men, as well as the services of a daring and able leader. Their arrival caused a slight change in the position of some of the regiments, but the general disposition of the army remained as before. The camp was now a very lively scene, and contained a strange mixture of uniforms and faces, which showed the motley nature of the force which had been scraped together in this desperate crisis of the empire. The well-known British scarlet was a rare sight indeed. The European regiments in India wear white clothing in the hot weather; but white is not well suited to campaigning, as the reader can conceive, and most of them had dyed their clothes the well-known *khakee* (or dust colour). This *khakee,* which before May, 1857, was only seen across the Indus, was a sort of grey drab, varying very much in tint, but adopted by the frontier troops for their hill fighting, being nearly the colour of the desert, or the bare stony hills in those parts, and therefore admirably suited to the constant skirmishing against men armed with matchlocks good at 600 yards' distance. Directly these troops marched to join our camp, the advantages of this colour were seen, and it quickly became fashionable for everybody, which it has pretty well since remained. Coke's 1st Punjab Infantry, and the Sirmoor Battalion of Goorkhas (perhaps the two finest Native corps in camp), had stuck, however, to their original green, which looked most wofully dilapidated by the service it had seen. Almost every other regiment (cavalry, artillery and infantry), Native and European, turned out in the aforesaid *khakee,* but it was of so many different shades, puce colour, slate colour, drab, &c., that a delightful variety was exhibited, not only in the uniforms of different corps, but (alas! for the native dyers) in men belonging to the same company. There certainly was little of the pomp, whatever there might be of the circumstance, of war at Delhi. As long as a man's weapon was in good fighting order, commanding officers did not trouble their heads very much about the dressing. As to the Staff and Engineer officers, I am quite sure no two men were dressed alike in the whole camp. Boots of all kinds,—top-boots, jack-boots, antigropellos, &c., with trowsers and breeches of every description, coats of every variety of colour and cut, and head-dresses, including the turban, the helmet, the solah-topee, the wide-awake, and half-a-dozen others, showed that utility had not been sacrificed to beauty. Indeed, it seemed pretty generally agreed that whatever in these matters had been the arrangements in time of peace, must inevitably be wrong in time of war, and I am not sure that the mistake was a great one.

The difference in physiognomies was greater almost than the varieties in dress. The pale or sunburnt European; the short, monkey-faced little Goorkha; the hardy-looking Pathan or north country Mussulman, with his high cheek-bones and often almost white face; the tall, soldierly Seikh, with his long hair twisted up behind; and the clean, well-made, handsome Poorbeah,—few though they were that had remained faithful to us,—with many other representations of tribes and castes, showed pretty well that the quarrel between the Feringhee Government and its mutinous Sepoys was certainly not viewed as a national quarrel. In fact (counting the camp followers), for every white man in camp there were certainly twenty black ones; and this one fact, natural and ordinary as it appeared to us all, often struck me as the most cheering omen of our real hold upon the country.

All this time, too, the camp was remarkably well supplied, principally owing to the exertions of that admirable commissariat which has never failed us in India. The men fed well, and the officers, too; very much better, in fact, than they did when (in spite of the crisis of the war being over) their mess supplies had run out, and there was no hope of replacing them; so that, hard as the work was, small as were our numbers, and terrible the struggle that lay before us, we should hardly have had credit for it by a Crimean officer, when he found champagne, hock, and claret flying about pretty freely at every mess in camp.

Nevertheless, the severity of the duty, the constant exposure, and the unhealthiness of the time of the year, told heavily upon the army. The reinforcements that had arrived scarcely supplied the drain caused by casualties and sickness. The European and Native regiments that had been fighting from the first were little more than skeleton regiments. All were looking forward with eagerness to the arrival of the siege train, and of the last few reinforcements that could be scraped together, to help us. Every one knew that their arrival would be the signal for work ten times as heavy, and exertions ten times as great, as any they had yet undergone. Nevertheless, it would be the beginning of the end, and few doubted what that end would be, however dear the price to be paid for it.

At length we heard that the siege train had left Phillour, had passed Umballa, and was on its way down: 50 pieces of heavy ordnance, and 800 carts laden with ammunition. But there was a very small escort with it, for there were scarcely any troops to send; and the enemy, knowing this as well as we did, determined on a bold stroke round our right flank, with the view of intercepting it, and capturing or destroying the convoy. A force of 10,000 men and 13 guns accordingly moved from the city, and marched to Nujufghur, whence they prepared to move round to our rear by a wide circuit. General Wilson at once despatched General Nicholson, with as strong a force as could be spared, to intercept them, and, if possible, bring them to action. On the night of the 24th of August the force left camp, and through a pouring rain, and over a country inundated with water, the troops marched on, with difficulty getting the guns along with them. At twelve o'clock the following day, a halt was ordered, and the General and his staff rode on to reconnoitre. He found the enemy awaiting him in a position of considerable strength. The troops, having slightly recovered from their fatigue, were brought up. The Horse Artillery galloped forward, unlimbered within 300 yards, and poured such a close and well-directed fire on the rebel guns, that in ten minutes they were all silenced. The Infantry then advanced and deployed into line, stormed a serai on the enemy's left, and then, changing front to the left, bore down everything before them. Only in one place was the resistance determined, where the 1st Punjab Rifles, in driving the enemy out of a village, suffered severely, losing their commanding officer, Lieut. Lumsden. The enemy lost the whole of his artillery, treasure, and camp equipage, and fled precipitately back to Delhi. The bridge over the Nujufghur drain, by which they had crossed, was blown up, and our victorious army returned to camp.

No further attempt was made to molest the siege guns, which, on the 3rd of September, safely arrived in camp. On the morning of the 7th, our last reinforcements arrived, in the shape of the 4th Punjab

Rifles (commanded by Captain A. Wilde), then and since one of the finest regiments in the service. They had come down from the Euxufzaie frontier, near Peshawur, at the rate of 25 miles a day, to take part in the great struggle, after doing excellent service in keeping that border quiet. As they marched into camp, with their short rifles at the trail, at a long swinging step, the Europeans turned out to admire the sturdy frames and fierce-looking faces under the Khakee turbans, and began to fraternize with the new regiment of "Sakes," or Seikhs, as the Punjabees were always called.

I went out to meet an old friend in the commandant, and recognized more than one familiar dark face in the regiment, which I had long known on the Derajat frontier.

Nothing could have been more satisfactory, and, at the same time, more ludicrous, than the way these men and the European soldiers fraternized together throughout the whole campaign. They were constantly sitting and talking together in the camp; though, as neither understood more than a word or two of the other's language, how they managed to keep up a conversation is difficult to comprehend. A European would come to see one of the native officers, perhaps, who would get up, offer his friend the only stool in his possession, and then sit down on his bed. Then the soldier would light his pipe, gravely puff away, and begin to talk, the other following suit; and each holding forth quite independently of his companion. Of course, this excellent understanding had the best possible effect, and I never heard of its being broken.

On the night of the 7th of September, we at last began the siege of Delhi.

CHAPTER VI.

THE SIEGE OF DELHI.

In describing the position occupied by the British army, I have explained that we had scarcely a choice as to the front to be attacked. The security gained by our left flank being placed on the river, and the covering of our only line of communication with the Punjab, were such important advantages to our small force, that they must have quite outweighed any considerations dependent on the relative strength of the attackable fronts, and pointed out the north side as the only one where we had a chance of success.

The resistance to be overcome did not, however, depend on the actual strength of the fortifications. The military reader will at once understand that the smallness of our force, and the great circumference of the walls, effectually precluded every idea of our investing the place. As at Sebastopol, then, so at Delhi, we fought under the disheartening reflection; our enemy under the great consolation of knowing that his retreat could not be cut off, and that supplies and reinforcements of all kinds could enter his camp quite as freely as ours.

Moreover, he possessed inside his walls a force at least treble our own, and the largest arsenal in India, containing 200 siege guns, and an inexhaustible supply of ammunition.

No one acquainted with these facts could shut his eyes to the difficulties of our position; but every one was aware that the attempt must be made without further delay, and that, if unsuccessful, our empire in India was for the time lost.

The rebellion had now steadily been gaining ground for four months, and no decisive check had as yet been given to it. The Seikh and other Native States, that had as yet stood by us, could hardly be expected to do so much longer, without some great success on our part. Disaffection had already appeared in the Bombay and Madras armies, and was likely to spread; and even the Punjab, on which alone we rested, was beginning to totter in its fidelity, shaken by the unaccountable delay that had occurred in restoring the prestige of our arms. No succours could be looked for from down country. We had heard the sad tale of the massacre of Cawnpore, and of Havelock's unavailing attempts to relieve the garrison of Lucknow, and every man in the Upper Provinces available for offensive operations was now before Delhi.

The plan of attack prepared by the Chief Engineer

and his second in command * was simple, bold, and effective, and I may honestly say that it was worked out by his subalterns with an energy and skill that have, I am sure, never been surpassed. In fact, had it not been for the indefatigable exertions of every branch of the service, and of every grade in it, success could not have been obtained in the face of such difficulties.

One great fault that had been committed by the enemy, in their defensive preparations, was promptly taken advantage of in the attack. Their bastions were the only part of their fortifications on which guns could be mounted. Their connecting curtains were merely parapets, wide enough only for a musketry fire. With the large amount of labour at their command, they might have easily rectified this, by pulling down the adjacent buildings, and on their ruins erecting a rampart, that would have enabled them to mount double or treble our number of guns; and they ought to have known that we must attack

* Captain Alexander Taylor, of the Bengal Engineers,—the Chief Engineer had been wounded by the splinter of a shell a little before the siege actually commenced, and though he still visited the trenches, the real management of the attack devolved upon Captain Taylor, who virtually directed the whole siege operations in the field from the commencement to their triumphant conclusion. No one, but his own brother officers, knew the great responsibility that devolved upon him, and the amount of anxiety, labour, and exposure, that he underwent in consequence.

them from the north side. But ignorant on this point, or from whatever other reason, they neglected this precaution; therefore we knew that if we could crush the fire of their bastions, and effect our breaches before they could rectify this blunder, we should nullify their immense superiority in artillery, and could launch the infantry against the town with confidence.

The light gun battery, mentioned above, having been established on the plateau to the left of the Sammy House, the first great step to be taken, after this preliminary one, was to crush the fire of the Moree Bastion at the N.W. corner of the city, so as to make our advance secure on the extreme left, where the breaches were to be formed.

A spirited address had just been issued to the troops by General Wilson, setting forth the importance of the operations about to be undertaken, and exhorting them to do their best to carry out the directions of the Engineers.

On the afternoon of the 7th, at the usual time, we were warned as to what officers would be required for the night's work, and found that nearly every available officer and man was told off, as it was intended to construct and arm the right batteries in one night.

At sunset, I proceeded to Hindoo Rao's, with Captain T——. to assist him in tracing No. 1 battery.

We went down to the ground which had been previously surveyed, as above described, accompanied by half a dozen Sappers, with tracing implements, and found the coast quite clear. Silently and quietly the battery was traced 700 yards from the work to be attacked. The right portion was to contain six guns to smash the Moree; the left portion, 200 yards distant, was for four guns, to keep down the fire of the Cashmere Bastion until we could attack it more directly; both portions were to be connected by a trench which, carried on, communicated with the deep nullah close to the rear, that was to be used as a first parallel. Just as the tracing was completed, down came the strong covering party, which was placed in front so as to support the videttes put out still further. In the meantime, the camels began to arrive with the fascines and gabions* required for the battery, and accompanied by the working parties, who were told off in dead silence, to their

* The ground was rocky, with a very slight coating of earth, and as we were short of men, and pressed for time, all the siege batteries at Delhi were constructed after a new fashion. The solid portion, up to the level of the embrasure, was constructed entirely of fascines; the merlons above of sand bags, previously filled; the embrasures and interior face of the merlons being reveted in the usual manner with gabions and fascines. These batteries were very rapidly constructed, and answered admirably, except they were highly inflammable, one of those made the first night being ignited from the fire of our own guns, and entirely destroyed.

separate portions of work. It was a bright starlight evening, the moon not rising till about ten o'clock.

The camels made the usual groaning and roaring while being unladen, and we would have given something to stop their mouths, but as that was impossible, we could only bear it with patience, and hope Pandy wouldn't hear it.

The moon rose on a busy scene: hundreds of camels arriving, dropping their loads, and returning; and hundreds of men, as busy as bees, raising up a formidable work, which was to be finished and ready to open fire in the morning,—otherwise its subsequent completion would have been no easy matter. My particular work was to construct the three magazines, which were to hold the powder required for the ten guns. All this time we had been perfectly unmolested by the enemy, and the work was progressing merrily, when suddenly a bright flash from the Moree, a loud report, and a heavy shower of grape, literally ploughed up the ground we were working on, knocking over several men. After a short interval, another, equally well-aimed shower, came down, and upset some more men, and the Engineers pulled long faces. If this sort of fun was to continue, we should lose half our men, and the idea of completing the battery that night must be abandoned. Singular to relate, however, Pandy, who, of course, couldn't tell how well he was shooting, seemed quite content, and only fired one more shot during the whole night; being, in fact, in perfect ignorance of what we were about. If he heard a noise, he probably thought it was one of our ordinary working parties cutting brushwood.

So, with a deep sigh of relief, the work went on rapidly. The night was very hot, but we had taken care to bring plenty of drink with us, and the excitement prevented any one feeling fatigued until the work was over. I went up to Hindoo Rao's, got some tea, and met the Artillery officer, who wanted to know when we should be ready for his guns. On returning, I found we had at length got rid of our camels; but now commenced arriving the long strings of artillery carts, laden with shot, shell, &c.; and as bullocks and bullock drivers are particularly stupid creatures, I am afraid there was a considerable amount of cursing and swearing, in getting these stores over the rough ground into the battery. Then came the huge guns, drawn by twenty pairs of bullocks each, and the sort of smothered row that ensued, beggars description. At three o'clock the place presented a scene of awful confusion. Sappers, pioneers, artillerymen, and infantry, all mixed up together with an inert mass of carts, guns, and bullocks struggling together in a heap. Scarcely another hour remained before daylight, and then we knew what we might expect from the irate enemy, when he saw what our amusement had been during the night. The confusion, however, was apparent, but not real: eveybody knew what his work was—and everybody did it. Men and officers worked like horses, and the chaotic mass of carts and animals cleared off to camp. The Artillery stowed their ammunition in the magazines, and as fast as our platforms were ready, the guns were dragged into their positions. Nevertheless, with all our exertions, we had only one gun ready for the Moree by the time that day began to dawn; the other five platforms, in that portion of the battery, being still incomplete. We were now obliged to let the great bulk of the working party go, as they were quite done up; and to have crossed the space between them and the camp, in open daylight, would have exposed them to certain destruction. I remained behind, however, with two other Engineers, to finish the remaining platforms. The covering party to the front was withdrawn, and the infantry supports, for the battery, were all kept under cover.

With the first break of day the enemy saw what we had been at, and then we *caught* it. The Moree Bastion sent round after round of shot and grape at us, so that almost every man who ventured from the protection of the battery was knocked over. The few workmen I had kept to finish the remaining platforms were quite cowed, and I was obliged to get volunteers from the Europeans. We had only one gun mounted to reply to this storm, until at length Major B——, the Artillery officer on command, dragged a howitzer well to the rear, and fired over the parapet. Pandy, finding his fire almost unchecked got very bold, and a large body of cavalry and infantry sallied forth from the Lahore Gate to attack the new battery; but they were fired into by the light guns on the plateau and all the ridge guns, and then got a dose of grape from us, so they made off quicker than they came. In the meantime, we had worked hard in the battery, and as each platform was finished, the artillery were able to open another gun on the enemy, until at length we felt their fire was slackening. Each shot told with tremendous effect, at this range, on the masonry Bastion, and the fire from the Moree became gradually feebler and feebler. I had done my work; but I waited for half an hour, not only to see the effect of our shooting, but because it was no joke to get across the intervening ground between us and the camp under such a fire; as soon, however, as it became somewhat fainter, I returned to my tent, about 8 a.m., thoroughly done up by the long night's work. By the afternoon the Moree had ceased to fire, and was a heap of ruins; but at no place did the enemy show such pluck, in standing to their guns, as at this Bastion, and to the last, whenever we gave them a little breathing time, they managed to get a gun into position, and treat us to a few doses, till they were again silenced. The severity of this day's work may be judged of, when I state that there were 70 casualties in the trenches.

The ground on the left had been taken possession of the day before, by the seizure of the Koodsea Bagh and Ludlow Castle, which were occupied by strong pickets. Pandy must have been taken by surprise, for he made no resistance, and for some time thought that our operations on the left were a mere feint, and that the real attack would be directed on the Moree.

On the evening of the 8th, strong working parties were sent down to make Battery No. 2, but we found from the previous night's experience that it would be too great a stretch of our available means to attempt again to complete the work in one night. I was told off again for work to-night, to commence Battery No. 3 on the extreme left; but as the site originally selected proved on closer examination to be faulty, it was necessary to postpone it for another day, and I was not sorry for the night's rest I enjoyed in con sequence.

Battery No. 2 was made in front of Ludlow Castle, 500 yards from the Cashmere Bastion. It was made in two portions; the right half for seven heavy howitzers and two 18-pounders. The left half, about 200 yards distant, was for nine 24-pounders. The whole of the eighteen guns were destined to silence the fire of the Cashmere Bastion, to knock away the parapet right and left that gave cover to the defenders, and to open the Main Breach, by which the town was to be stormed, which was to be made immediately to the left of the Bastion.

The working parties were not much molested, and about half the battery was finished during the night.

On the following evening, I was sent down with two other officers and a strong working party to finish the right half of No. 2, the left half being entrusted to another party.

I went down to the trenches about 5 p.m., to find the directing Engineer, and see what had to be done; the other officers following behind with the workmen as soon as it was dusk.

I found the directing Engineer at the Koodsea Bagh, into which a fair supply of shot and shell was being thrown by the enemy, and the trees were getting well peppered, most of the firing being high. Our men, however, who had got quite accustomed to it, were eating their dinners very comfortably, inside the different gateways and buildings which gave them shelter. G——, the Directing Engineer, and myself, went across to Ludlow Castle, and laid out the embrasures for the battery; Pandy, who was skirmishing in the broken ground in front, making shocking bad shots at us.

A little before dark the working party came down, and we all went to work like men to complete the battery by morning, which we did sufficiently to have enabled it to open fire had it been required to do so. But the other batteries being delayed, and it being thought advisable to open all on the left together, our guns did not fire in the morning. It was very hot work, standing or walking about all night, but we had plenty of claret, which is a comforting drink in such a case. In the middle of the night down came the guns, and we hauled them in behind the solid parts of the battery till the platforms were ready. The embrasures were then masked in front, so that the whole thing looked innocent enough from the outside.

This night also a battery was made in a safe spot in the Koodsea Bagh itself, for ten heavy mortars, which were soon ready to open fire when required.

I have said above that the site first chosen for the left breaching battery was found to be bad. In looking out for another, the director of the attack, after quietly searching for some time, and finding himself unobserved, at length discovered a small ruined building, which had been an out office of the Custom House. This Custom House was a large building, only 160 yards from the left or Water Bastion, and the enemy, with the most unaccountable negligence, had not destroyed it, nor were they occupying it. Of course, we immediately took possession of it, and it was determined to make the battery inside the aforesaid office, the front wall of which would effectually conceal our work, and give a sort of protection to the workmen. This same night, accordingly, the work had been begun; but to make a battery 160 yards from an enemy, with his men lining the walls, within easy musket shot, was a task that required no ordinary nerve and skill to resolve on and carry out. Pandy did not know what we were at, but at any rate he knew the people were working in that direction, and he served out such a liberal supply of musketry and shell that night, that the working party lost thirty-nine men killed and wounded. It was wonderful, indeed, to see with what courage the men worked.

They were merely the unarmed Native Pioneers I described above, and not meant to be fighting men. With the passive courage so common to Natives, as man after man was knocked over, they would stop a moment, weep a little over their fallen friend, pop his body in a row along with the rest, and then work on as before. Of course, at daylight, this, like all the working parties, was withdrawn, or every man must have been destroyed.

On the night of the 10th, I was again sent down to strengthen and complete the howitzer battery on which I had been employed the previous night. T——y, of the Engineers, was with me, and we had a working party from two of the European regiments, as no Sappers or Pioneers could be spared.

The men, however, were exhausted with the heat and hard work, and I was obliged to let them go at midnight, with the work still incomplete. However, the Directing Engineer then sent me 120 men of the Cashmere Contingent that had just joined us. They came down armed to the teeth with matchlocks, swords, and shields, and did not much fancy being ordered to pile arms, and to fill and carry sandbags, so we just set to work ourselves to set them the example, the native officer followed suit, and the men soon worked right well. About half-past three or four o'clock, however, the enemy suddenly opened a rattling fire of musketry on us from the ground in front; and, before I could stop them, my valiant workmen flew to their arms, and opened such a fire from their matchlocks in return, that, being in front, I expected to be shot dead every minute.

As the only way of stopping this abominable row, we forcibly ejected them from the cover of the parapet, telling them to fire away in the open if they wanted to fight, but that the battery was made for guns, and not for infantry.

The Artillery officers had now come down with their men to open fire in the morning, and having dragged the guns on to the platforms, we had now to unmask the embrasures, and I called for volunteers from the Dograhs, who cheerfully came forward and upset the sandbags that covered the guns behind; and though Pandy did not shoot badly for the ten minutes we were thus exposed, no one was hit.

Meanwhile, the left portion of this battery, containing the 24-pounders, had also been completed, and was ready to open. The heavy mortars under Major T——, of the Artillery, had been playing away all night on the line of works between the Cashmere and Water Bastions especially; and very pretty it was to watch the course of shell after shell, traceable by its lighted fuze, from the first *bang* when it left the mortar, to the thundering report when it fell and burst amongst the enemy.

The right battery, too, fired away, as it had been doing all along, and Pandy kept up such a row with shot, shell, musketry, and rockets, that the sight was as good as a fireworks exhibition at Vauxhall, with the additional charm of the risk of being killed, and having nothing to pay for your fun.

No. 3 Battery was still unfinished, and would not be ready until the following day; but it was not thought necessary to wait for it, and No. 2, the great breaching battery of eighteen guns, was ordered to open at once.

A delay of an hour or two occurred from some unavoidable cause, and the enemy in the Cashmere Bastion, seeing our embrasures unmasked, and eighteen guns grinning at him, but not firing, evidently determined to make the most of his respite. So at us he went with a right good will, sending grape and round shot into the bastion, and musketry from the ground in front.

In fact, he had not been idle while we had been working. As soon as he clearly perceived that we meant mischief on the left, he commenced to do what he ought to have done before, viz., to mount guns behind his long curtain; and so nearly, too, were they being ready, that had the subsequent assault been delayed for forty-eight hours, I believe we could not have assaulted at all, but must have been driven from our batteries, or had our men knocked to pieces there. Though these heavy guns, however, could not be got ready in a day, there were several convenient nooks out of the reach of our shot, and in these he mounted light guns, which annoyed us terribly by their oblique fire. Moreover, taking advantage of the broken ground before him, he had in one night made a long trench, covering the whole of the front, from which he now, till the end of the siege, kept up a rain of bullets, which never ceased by night or day, and, in spite of the cover of the batteries, caused us very many casualties.

CHAPTER VII.

THE SIEGE (CONTINUED).

At eight o'clock on the morning of the 11th, the great breaching battery opened fire. A salvo from the nine 24-pounders was followed by three tremendous cheers from the Artillery in the battery. As the site of the breach was struck with the iron hail, great blocks of stone fell, and the curtain wall fell clattering into the ditch. The howitzers soon after followed suit. In ten minutes, the Cashmere bastion was silenced; and then it was a fine sight to see the stone-work crumbling under the storm of shot and shell, the breach getting larger and larger, and the 8-inch shells, made to burst just as they touched the parapet, bringing down whole yards of it at a time.

I waited to see the batteries open fire, and then returned to camp, regularly tired out, having been up for the last two nights. Now that the batteries were finished, it was decided that an Engineer officer should be constantly present in them, to be relieved every twenty-four hours, so as to keep them in efficient working order. I was to take my first turn of this duty in the Howitzer Battery, at 5 a.m. on the following day, the 12th.

The guns fired all day long on the 11th; but the men, being quite exhausted, did not fire much during the night, leaving the work to the mortars; and the ten heavy and twelve light mortars kept up such an infernal fire of shells along the whole front, that Pandy must have found it anything but pleasant. This night, also (the 11th and 12th), No. 3 Battery was nearly completed, and would open the following day with six 18-pounders, to breach the Water Bastion, or rather the adjoining curtain.

It had been found very troublesome removing the old walls of the building inside which, as I have said, this battery was constructed, and the distance being so close, so hot a fire was maintained on the working parties, that our casualties were heavy, and the delay greater than had been anticipated.

On the morning of the 12th, I went down to the Howitzer Battery, as the Engineer on duty, and remained there until the following morning, and a more unpleasant twenty-four hours I never spent in my life. The enemy, now thoroughly alive to his danger, lined his advanced trenches with men, and threw crowds of skirmishers over the broken ground and jungle in front, who maintained one incessant storm of musketry into the batteries all day long, rendering it most dangerous to venture, even for a minute, beyond the protection of the parapets. Every now and then they were so annoying, and became so bold, that the Artillery officers substituted grape for round shot in the guns, and ploughed up the ground in front with the iron shower. The ground, however, was so favourable for the enemy, that this only checked their approach, and scarcely diminished the severity of their fire. The light guns they had got to play on us from the Martello Towers, and from holes knocked in the curtain walls, also caused great annoyance, as they fired at us with perfect impunity, we having no guns to reply to them. A shell from one of these, in the course of the day, burst in the battery, and severely wounded five of the men, two of whom, I believe, died. Many men fell from the musketry. I was twice hit by splinters of stones thrown into the battery, by a round shot striking a low wall outside; and the narrow escapes that all had were numerous. But a more serious annoyance than all these yet remains to be described. The enemy had constructed a battery beyond our extreme right, and so well placed, that our old ridge guns could not see it, and from this he enfiladed No. 1 and 2 Batteries with fearful effect. The fire in front could be seen and replied to, but it was very trying to the nerves to see the battery raked from end to end, almost every half hour, by an 18-pounder's round shot, which came tearing through, upsetting everything in its course, and smashing many a brave fellow. I lengthened the right epaulment, and constructed an additional traverse, which somewhat protected us; but the fire was still so severe, that at length we had to withdraw a gun from playing on the breach, and put it in the epaulment, to keep down the enfilade fire if possible. General Wilson, in fact, at one time determined to make a rush at these guns from the right, and spike or capture them; but they were within grape shot of the walls, were difficult to get at, and the loss of life would probably have been heavy; whereas, if our artillerymen could only hold on for another twenty-four hours, it was hoped the work would be done.

At 11 a.m., the left or No. 3 Battery was at length finished, and ready to open fire. The task of unmasking the embrasures, in broad daylight, and under a close musketry fire from the walls, was done in the bravest manner by G——, of the Engineers, and some of our Poorbeah Sappers, and in another minute the six guns opened fire. The effect of these heavy guns playing, at 160 yards' distance, on the Water Bastion was tremendous. The enemy's guns were dismounted or smashed almost immediately; the opposing face of the bastion was beaten into a shapeless mass, the parapet sent flying about in fragments, and the breach seemed, in a few hours, almost practicable. But though the enemy could not show a gun in reply, he poured such a close and hot musketry fire into the work from the walls, at that short distance, that the air seemed literally alive with bullets. To enter the battery from the Koodsea Bagh picket was a service of great danger, though the distance to be run was scarcely 100 yards. Fortunately, a dip in the ground screened us somewhat. Many valuable lives were lost in this hot post; foremost amongst them, the brave Fagan, of the Artillery, who received a bullet through the brain, whilst working one of the guns.

This battery was also exposed to an enfilade fire from Pandy's guns across the river; though, on account of the distance, not to anything like the extent the others suffered from the fire on the right. But all were more or less fired into from the front and on both flanks, and never were guns better or more unflinchingly served. Exhausted by the heat, and worn out by the constant work and exposure, the Artillery officers and men felt that the army was waiting for them to beat down the walls that had looked defiantly at us so long, and to open a road for them into Delhi. Undismayed by the terrible list of casualties from the enemy's fire, they poured an uninterrupted storm of shot and shell on the devoted fortifications; and, in spite of the vigour of the defence, we saw that every gun, howitzer, and mortar was effecting its object.

To return to my own ground. We had yet another danger to guard against—that from fire. All the batteries were very inflammable, from their peculiar formation, and several times took fire from the discharge of our own guns. Of course, it was the Engineer's duty, when this took place, to jump on the parapet, or stand in the embrasures, and put it out, for which purpose we had chatties of water kept ready filled. I had to do this six or eight times; and there was a strange kind of excitement about it, as you knew that every musket within range was turned on you at the time, which quite took away any fear, though it made one very glad to jump down again on to the platform.

So the day wore on. The heat was very great, but the excitement of the scene almost prevented its being felt. The men's dinner and beer came into the batteries, and were heartily enjoyed; and, in the evening, sundry scared figures in white came running into the place, one by one, and proved to be our *khidmutgars*, bringing the officers' dinners. And it is only fair to this much-abused class of servants to record how bravely they behaved in this respect. There were very few who, even when their masters' posts were the most dangerous, ever hesitated to bring them their dinners, as regularly as clockwork.

The *bheesties* were another class of servants that behaved equally well. In the many conflicts that took place outside the walls of Delhi, these men, with their water-bags, always kept up with the European troops, and were ready with their cooling draught in the heat of the battle, and many of them lost their lives or their limbs on these occasions. The European soldiers duly appreciated this pluck. When it was war to the knife with every other Pandy, the rebel bheesties were spared, out of compliment to heir fraternity; and many a windfall of loot from the bodies of the slain did our regimental bheesties get hold of, by the favour of the Europeans. After discussing our dinners, pipes were lighted, and the officer commanding in the battery made arrangements for a mild sort of firing to be kept up through the night; while the artillery, in general, lay down to sleep away their day's fatigue. So thoroughly did one get accustomed to the row, and so great was the fatigue, that the regular discharge of the guns fired through the night, within ten feet of the sleeper, would not disturb his repose. Meanwhile, my working party for the night had come down, and the damage done to the embrasures by the day's firing was repaired before the morning. Pandy's fire always slackened very much at night, though it never ceased, so we worked away very comfortably. And at 5 a.m., L——, of the Engineers, came down to take *his* twenty-four hours; and I departed to camp, glad enough to find myself with a whole skin, when so many had been knocked over, and to have some hours' rest before encountering fresh fatigues. This was the morning of the 13th. All this day the two breaching batteries maintained their tremendous fire, and the enemy, in return, kept up a still hotter fire than before on the batteries. Our casualties were numerous, and the artillerymen thoroughly exhausted. The enemy might open fresh guns on us from behind the curtain, where we knew he was busy at work. The enfilade fire on the right might be so considerably increased as to render our batteries no longer tenable. It was hoped, therefore, that by this evening the breaches would be practicable, so that the assault could be delivered on the following morning. The arrangements for the assault had already been made by the General, in concert with the Chief Engineer, and were communicated in writing to the different Commanding Officers.

About 3 p.m., when sound asleep, I was sent for by the Chief Engineer, and told to go down and examine the main breach, near the Cashmere Bastion, and see if it were practicable. I was first to go and look at the ground in the afternoon, and make my own arrangements for the expedition. I got a note to the officer commanding at the Koodsea Bagh picket, to give me what men I required to go with me; and I also took notes to the officers commanding the batteries, requesting them to cease firing when I should send word.

I was to get as close to the breach as possible, to get down into the ditch, and even up to the top of the breach, if it could be done, to see if there were any guns in the flank defending the breach, if the counterscarp of the ditch could be descended without ladders; and, in a word, report if the breach was practicable for immediate assault.

As I knew pretty well the section of the wall and ditch, I first went to the park and ordered a short light bamboo ladder to be made, capable of being carried by two men, with which to ascend the masonry escarp. I then went down to the Koodsea Bagh to examine the ground. Leaving my horse at the last safe place on the road, I went into the batteries, and found that L——, of the Engineers, had just been sent, in the dusk of the evening, on the same errand as myself, by the director of the attack, Captain T——. He soon returned, however, having been seen, fired at, and compelled to retreat. I therefore decided, as this attempt had probably put the enemy on the *qui vive*, that it would be better not to make another attempt earlier than ten o'clock, L—— agreeing to go with me, as he now knew the way, and we could take the men who went with him. I found we could advance straight towards the breach from the Custom House, through a garden and jungle, which would give us cover till we were within sixty yards of the breach. Then we should have to advance in the open; we should pass the extremity of the enemy's advanced trench, and thus leave all the skirmishers on our right rear. I therefore went to the officers commanding the batteries, and requested them to fire heavily on the breach until ten o'clock, and then to cease firing, as the attempt would at that hour be made. We then returned to the Koodsea Bagh, and arranged with the officer commanding that six picked riflemen, belonging to H.M.'s 60th Rifles, should accompany us, and that an officer and twenty men of the same regiment should follow in support, and should be left at the edge of the jungle while we went on to the breach. If he saw that we were being cut off, he was to come up to our support, and sound his whistle to us to fall back. If we had a man wounded, or wanted his support, we would, in like manner, whistle for him.

These preliminaries being arranged, and the ladder having arrived from the park, we sat down quietly at the picket, and ate our dinners.

It was a bright starlight night, with no moon, and the roar of the batteries, and clear, abrupt reports of the shells from the mortars, alone broke the stillness of the scene, while the flashes of the rockets, carcases, and fireballs lighting up the air ever and anon, made a really beautiful spectacle. Just then, however, an 8-inch shell from the enemy buried itself in the ground close to where we were sitting, and bursting (luckily for us, well below the surface), covered the whole party with a shower of earth, and made us scramble away in most admired confusion. The *ghurees* struck ten, and the fire of the batteries suddenly ceased. Our party was in readiness; we drew swords, felt that our revolvers were ready to hand, and leaving the shelter of the picket, such as it was, advanced stealthily into the enemy's country.

Creeping quietly through the garden mentioned above, we quickly found ourselves under a large tree, on the edge of the cover, and here we halted for a moment, conversing only in whispers. The enemy's skirmishers were firing away on our right some thirty yards from us, and the flashes of their muskets lit up the air as if they had been fireflies. The shells and rockets of the enemy at one moment illumined the space around, as they sailed over our heads, and then left us in total darkness. We now left the Rifle officer, Lieutenant H——, and his twenty men in support, and with the six men who were to accompany us, L—— and I emerged into the open, and pushed straight for the breach. In five minutes we found ourselves on the edge of the ditch, the dark mass of the Cashmere Bastion immediately on the other side, and the breach distinctly discernible. Not a soul was in sight. The counterscarp was sixteen feet deep, and steep; L—— slid down first, I passed down the ladder, and taking two men out of the six, descended after him, leaving the other four on the top to cover our retreat. Two minutes more and we should have been at the top of the breach; but quiet as we had been, the enemy was on the watch, and we heard several men running from the left towards the breach. We therefore reascended, though with some difficulty, and throwing ourselves down on the grass, waited in silence for what was to happen. A number of figures immediately appeared on the top of the breach, their forms clearly discernible against the bright sky, and not twenty yards distant. We, however, were in the deep shade, and they could not apparently see us. They conversed in a low tone, and presently we heard the ring of their steel ramrods as they loaded. We waited quietly, hoping they would go away, when another attempt might be made. Meanwhile we could see that the breach was a good one, the slope easy of ascent, and that there were no guns in the flank. We knew by experience, too, that the ditch was easy of descent. It was, however, desirable, if possible, to get to the top, but the sentries would not move. At one time the thought occurred to me of attempting the ascent by force. We might have shot two or three of them from where we lay, and in the surprise the rest might have run, and we could have been to the top and back before they had seen how small our party was; but the extreme hazard of the attempt, and the utter impossibility of rescuing any one that might be wounded in the ditch, made me abandon the idea, when I further reflected that we had, in reality, gained all the needful information. After waiting therefore some minutes longer, I gave a signal, the whole of us jumped up at once, and ran back towards our own ground. Directly we were discovered, a volley was sent after us; the balls came whizzing about our ears, but no one was touched. We reached our support in safety, and all quietly retreated to the Koodsea Bagh by the same road we had come. L—— went off to the batteries to tell them they might open fire again, and I got on to my horse and galloped back to camp as hard as I could, to make my report to the Chief Engineer—the roar of the batteries, as I rode off, showing that they had once more opened fire on the breach.

I found the Chief Engineer in his office; drew out my report on paper, with a sketch of the breach, which I reported practicable for immediate assault. The left breach, near the Water Bastion, had also been examined by G—— and H——, of the Engineers. It was reported practicable also; but the musketry parapets had not been so thoroughly destroyed as could be done if a little more time was allowed, and another twenty-four hours' firing would have greatly *improved* it. But the danger of delay, for many reasons, and the worn out state of the artillery in the batteries, determined the Chief Engineer to advise the general assault to be delivered at daybreak the next morning. A note to this effect was at once sent off to General Wilson; and I again rode back to the batteries to call in our officers on duty, to be ready at their posts, with the different columns.

The arrangements for the assault had all been previously made, and the General's order being at once issued for the columns to fall in at three o'clock, the whole camp was soon astir. It was close upon three before I returned again from the batteries. I was so thoroughly tired, that I would have given much for an hour's rest; but the excitement soon took away the fatigue. In another half hour I was with my column, which was to storm the main breach, and joining General Nicholson and Captain T——, found myself marching to the assault on Delhi.

CHAPTER VIII.

THE ASSAULT.

THE programme of the assault was as follows, with the names of the Engineers attached:—

1st Column, Brigadier-General Nicholson.—H.M.'s 75th Regiment; 1st Bengal Fusileers; 2nd Punjab Infantry. To storm the breach near the Cashmere Bastion, and escalade the face of the bastion. Engineer officers attached, Lieuts. Medley, Lang, and Bingham.

2nd Column, Brigadier Jones, C.B.—H.M.'s 8th Regiment; 2nd European Bengal Fusileers; 4th Seikh Infantry. To storm the breach in the Water Bastion. Engineer officers attached, Lieuts. Greathed, Hovenden, and Pemberton.

3rd Column, Colonel Campbell.—H.M.'s 52nd Regiment; Kumaon Battalion; 1st Punjab Infantry. To assault by the Cashmere Gate, after it should be blown open. Engineer officers attached, Lieuts. Home, Salkeld, and Tandy.

4th Column, Major Reid.—Detachment of European Regiments; Sirmoor Battalion; Detachment of Dograhs. To attack the suburb Kissengunge, and enter the Lahore Gate. Engineer officers attached, Lieuts. Maunsell and Tennant.

5th Column, Brigadier Longfield.—H.M.'s 60th Rifles; Belooch Battalion; 4th Punjab Infantry. The reserve to follow the 1st Column. Engineer officers attached, Lieuts. Ward and Thackeray.

The assault, it will be seen, was to be delivered at four separate points. Of these, three were on the left of our position, directed on the face we had been attacking. The fourth was to be delivered from Hindoo Rao's house, on the right, against the suburbs of Kissengunge and Paharipore, from which the enemy were to be expelled, and their enfilading guns taken. This would secure the flank of our principal attack, and cause a powerful diversion. It was entrusted to Major Reid, who had held command of the right flank along the ridge ever since the arrival of the army in June.

Of the three attacks on the left, two were directed against the breaches near the Cashmere and Water Bastions, while the 3rd Column was to enter by the Cashmere Gate itself, which was to be blown open by an explosion party sent on ahead. It was at first intended that the blowing open of the gate should be the signal for the general assault. But this was afterwards altered, and the three columns advanced simultaneously.

The troops fell in, in perfect silence, on the high road leading from cantonments to the city,—the scaling ladders at the head of the columns. Some unavoidable delay took place, which detained the advance, and it was already day-dawn when the columns got fairly in motion.

My place was at the head of the 1st Division, 1st Column, which I was to guide to the attack on the main breach, the scene of our nocturnal expedition. L——, who had accompanied me on that occasion, was to head the 2nd Division of the same column, to escalade the face of the adjoining bastion.

The advance to the assault was a sight not to be forgotten. The sullen roar of our batteries, which fired with redoubled fury, to cover the advance of the troops; the noise of the answering shells, rockets, and round shot from the enemy, as they burst, or hissed, or rushed over our heads, lighting up the dark but clear atmosphere with lurid flashes; and the silent, steady tramp of the columns, as they advanced,—all made a scene which filled one with a mixture of awe and anxiety, and formed a striking contrast to the maddening excitement which so quickly followed it. All felt that the hour had at length come for which we had waited so long, and which had been so anxiously looked for, for months, in India and in England. All felt that on the events of that day depended (at least, temporarily) our hold on the empire of India; and though few, perhaps, knew the severity of the task before them, all went in with a stern determination to win.

I had not, however, much time for such reflections; my own particular work taking up most of my thoughts, and an intense anxiety lest anything should go wrong for which I was responsible, pretty well absorbing every other feeling in my mind. General Nicholson, who led the 1st Column, and had the general management of the attack, looked quiet but anxious. General Wilson rode up as we were advancing, and was also evidently full of anxiety.

Opposite Ludlow Castle the columns halted; those who were riding dismounted. I arranged my ladder men in front, took my place at their head, and the 1st Column, getting the word "Quick march," wheeled sharp to the left, and marched into the Koodsea Bagh, where we waited till all was ready for the signal.

The 2nd Column went on further to the left, and formed up in readiness behind No. 3 Battery, ready to dash on towards the left breach.

The 3rd Column remained on the high road, ready to advance on the Cashmere Gate. General Nicholson arranged that the signal for the assault should be the sudden advance of the 60th Rifles to the front, who were to cover the heads of the columns in skirmishing order. Captain T—— took me on with him to show me the exact ground over which the 1st Division was to advance towards the breach; and, stealing to the front, we advanced close to the edge of the jungle by the road that I had gone the previous night. He then left me to join the General, and at the same moment I heard a loud cheer. The Rifles dashed forward at a run, and, throwing themselves into the jungle, opened a sharp fire on the enemy on the walls.

This was the signal. Instantly, the head of my column appeared in sight, and I waved my sword for the ladder men to advance. Our batteries had, of course, ceased firing. A furious rattle of musketry was already pouring from the walls, and through a storm of bullets we steadily advanced at a quick walk, until we got to the edge of the cover. Then, forming the ladders into a sort of line, we rushed towards the breach, closely followed by the storming party, and, in a minute, found ourselves on the edge of the ditch. But so terrific was the fire from the breach and the broken parapet walls, that it was at first impossible to get the ladders down into the ditch, which was necessary to enable us to ascend the masonry escarp below the breach. Man after man was struck down, and the enemy, with yells and curses, kept up a terrific fire, even catching up stones from the breach in their fury, and, dashing them down, dared us to come on. At this moment I felt a shock, like a blow, on my right arm, which made me stagger, and then I knew I was wounded,—a ball having passed through the upper part of the arm, just shaving the bone. The excitement was, however, too great for pain to be felt, and I knew that the bone had escaped, so that it could not much matter.

The check on the edge of the ditch was but momentary; the storming parties pushed on, two ladders were thrown into the ditch, and a brave officer, Fitzgerald, of H.M.'s 75th Regiment, who was killed directly afterwards, was the first to mount. As soon as I saw my first ladder down, I slid down into the ditch, mounted up the escarp, and scrambled up the breach, followed by the soldiers.

Pandy never attempted to stand when he saw we really meant to close with him. The breach was won, and the supporting troops pouring in fast, went down the ramp into the main guard below.

It is now time to revert to the proceedings of the other columns up to this point.

No. 2, bravely led by Greathed and Hovenden, of the Engineers, who marched ahead with the ladder party, emerged from the cover of No. 3 Battery, and advanced towards the Water Bastion. They had to make a slight detour to the right, to avoid some water in the ditch; but so fierce was the musketry from the walls, that both the Engineers were struck down, severely wounded; and of the ladder men, consisting of thirty-nine men, twenty-nine were rendered *hors de combat* in a few minutes. Eventually, however, the ladders were placed, and the breach carried with a rush; but a large number of the storming party, straying too far to the right, went in at the main breach.

No. 3 Column advanced to the turn in the road leading to the Cashmere Gate, and halted while the explosion party went on to blow in the gate. It was intended that this dangerous operation should be done just as the day broke, but, from the delay that had arisen, it was now broad daylight; and the operation was, therefore, one of fearful hazard.

The explosion party consisted of Lieutenants Home and Salkeld, of the Engineers; Sergeants Carmichael, Burgess, and Smith, of the Bengal Sappers, and eight Native Sappers to carry the bags of powder. A bugler of H.M.'s 52nd (Hawthorne) also accompanied the party, to sound the advance when the gate was blown in.

There was an outer barrier gate which was found open, and Lieutenant Home then advanced over the broken drawbridge across the ditch with four men, each carrying a bag of twenty-five pounds of powder, which was deliberately laid at the foot of the great double gate. So utterly paralyzed were the enemy at the audacity of the proceeding, that they only fired a few straggling shots, and made haste to close the wicket with every appearance of alarm, so that Lieutenant Home, after laying his bags, jumped into the ditch unhurt. It was now Salkeld's turn. He also advanced with four other bags of powder, and a lighted port-fire. But the enemy had now recovered their consternation, and had seen the smallness of the party, and the object of their approach. A deadly fire was poured upon the little band from the top of the gateway from both flanks, and from the open wicket not ten feet distant. Salkeld laid his bags, but was shot through the arm and leg, and fell back on the bridge, handing the port-fire to Sergeant Burgess, bidding him light the fusee. Burgess was instantly shot dead in the attempt. Sergeant Carmichael then advanced, took up the port-fire, and succeeded in the attempt, but immediately fell, mortally wounded. Sergeant Smith, seeing him fall, advanced at a run, but finding that the fuse was already burning, threw himself down into the ditch, where the bugler had already conveyed poor Salkeld. In another moment a terrific explosion shattered the massive gate. The bugle sounded the advance, and with a loud cheer the 52nd charged through the broken gateway.

Thus was accomplished one of the most daring acts probably on record. Salkeld, Home, Sergeant Smith, and Bugler Hawthorne received the Victoria Cross from General Wilson. But poor Salkeld, after lingering several days, died of his wounds; and the gallant Home, after his hair-breadth escape, met death accidentally soon afterwards, while blowing up the Fort of Malagurh.

The 4th Column, under Major Reid, marched from Hindoo Rao's at daylight to the attack of Paharipore. Advancing from the Subzee Mundee, they successfully made their way to within 200 yards of the enemy's principal battery, whence they had to turn left, and by a rush would have taken the guns in rear; but the enemy were well prepared, a terrible fire from the streets and houses of this crowded suburb struck down, among others, at the same moment the Commanding Officer and the Senior Engineer. The troops of the Cashmere Contingent were staggered by the pitiless storm. No other officer was well acquainted with the localities of the place, and, after the most strenuous exertions of the European officers, the column was compelled to retreat, covered by the Goorkhas of Reid's Battalion in their usual cool manner.

To return to the left attack. Directly the troops got inside, General Nicholson got the great body of them together in the square of the main guard, and then at the head of the first column turned to the right, and advanced along the foot of the walls towards the Lahore Gate. Though beaten from the walls, the enemy still held the numerous and lofty houses all around, from which they maintained an unceasing rattle of musketry, while the Selimgurh and the Palace (the old and new citadels) treated us to plentiful supplies of shot and shell.

We were now at one end of the town, and our flank attack on the right having failed, nothing remained but to advance to the front, and drive the enemy gradually before us through the other end.

Captain T——, seeing I was wounded, desired me not to go on with the first column, but to stay and clear the Cashmere Gate, so as to admit the light guns which were to help the advance. This I did after some trouble, the effects of the explosion having only brought down one-half of the gate, and choked the passage with rubbish. Several dead bodies of the enemy who had perished in the explosion were lying there, scorched and smouldering, a horrible sight. The gateway became quickly thronged with artillery and ammunition pressing in, and the Doolies bearing the wounded and dying streaming out,—most of the sufferers quiet and insensible from loss of blood, others groaning in agony; and some came staggering up, supported by their comrades, the leaden hue of the countenance, and fixed, glazed expression of the eye, telling that they were struck in a vital part, and had but a short time to live.

Nos. 1 and 2 Columns, meanwhile, had cleared the ramparts of the flying army, and seized the Moree Bastion; but in the attempt to advance beyond this to the next bastion, commanding the Lahore Gate at the entrance to the Chandee Chouk, the deadly fire from the houses in the narrow street made the men recoil. General Nicholson went to the front to cheer them on, when he fell, mortally wounded, and was with difficulty carried back into camp. The troops then retired to the Cabul Gate, just beyond the Moree Bastion.

The reserve column advanced on the open suburbs, driving the enemy from the Church and from Skinner's House, but were pulled up at the Magazine, which the enemy held in force, and maintained a severe fire from its walls, turrets, and the adjoining houses. The 3rd Column took possession of the College, after a sharp struggle, and then advanced to attack the Jumma Musjid; but from the high terrace of this famous building, and from its courtyard walls, the enemy made a determined stand. The light guns were not yet up, and the column finally retreated, so that its head remained in a line with Nos. 1 and 2 on the right, and No. 5 on the left of it. We held the city from the north face to the canal, about one-fourth of the whole, but no farther. The cavalry, under Brigadier Grant, with nine Horse Artillery guns, who had been moved down at the commencement of the assault to check any sorties that might be attempted from the Lahore Gate, suffered severely from the fire of the Burn Bastion, remaining unflinchingly at their post until the infantry had established their position inside the town, when, being no longer required, they were withdrawn to Ludlow Castle.

The greater portion of the inhabitants had fled, and there were none of the deeds of horror to be seen that so often attend the capture of a city by storm. Nevertheless, a great deal of the usual disorder took place; the men of different columns and regiments got mixed up together. Shops and houses were broken open and completely gutted, and stores of beer, champagne, and brandy were found, and quickly appropriated by the thirsty soldiers.

I left the Cashmere Gate as soon as it was cleared, and went off to see what was going on in front. General Wilson had just ridden in, and, map in hand, was despatching officers to discover what we had and what we had not taken. Passing the English church, which was pretty well riddled with shot, I went on to the magazine, where I found a rapid exchange of firing going on between the enemy and our men. I found there was no advancing beyond this point, and feeling now faint and sick from my wound, I turned back, and walked towards the camp. As I passed out of the Cashmere Gate, I met two of my servants pressing in laden with the materials for a cold breakfast, and sundry bottles of lemonade, which my careful head-servant had despatched after me, as soon as he heard that the troops had got inside. I have seldom had a more refreshing drink than that. The second bottle I bestowed on an unfortunate wounded man with his thigh shattered by a bullet, and he thanked me with a most eloquent look. My syce and horse were standing quietly where I had left them four hours before, and the Doolies were evidently all occupied, so I rode quietly back to camp to find the doctor. An interminable line of Doolies was streaming down the road, filled with the wounded, and for hours the melancholy procession continued. But I knew not till afterwards at what a fearful cost our successes had been purchased—66 officers and 1,104 men had fallen in less than six hours something like one-third of the whole number engaged. The Engineer Brigade had suffered severely; out of 17 officers on duty, 10 were struck down—1 being shot dead, and 1 dying of his wounds.

I found our Doctor at the General Hospital, and then heard, as he exclaimed on seeing my bandaged arm, "What! another of you?" that I was the eighth Engineer officer that had already claimed his good offices to-day. I got my wound dressed, went over to my tent, and was soon sound asleep, after such a night and morning of fatigue and excitement as I am not likely to spend again.

To return, however, to what will interest the reader more than my personal adventures.

Our position in the city, though satisfactory to a certain extent, was still very hazardous. From the attack on the Paharipore suburb having failed, neither our right flank nor our camp was very secure. Though three columns out of four had partially succeeded in their attacks, they had still been stopped in their progress, and beaten back; and with so weak a force, and after our heavy losses, it was no joke to have to defend such an extensive position as we now held.

The Engineers, however, who were still fit for duty, went to work to secure our advanced position. Barricades were thrown up, the commanding houses made defensible with loopholes and parapets of sand-bags, and strong pickets, with videttes thrown out, kept up the flank communication between the heads of the three columns.

CHAPTER IX.

TERMINATION OF THE SIEGE.

ALL the next day was employed in thus securing our position, in restoring order, and putting a stop to indiscriminate plundering. Mortar batteries were also established to shell the city, the palace, and the Selimgurh; and a breach was made in the outer wall of the magazine.*

Early on the 16th the magazine was stormed and taken by H.M.'s 61st Regiment, the 4th Punjab Rifles, and the Belooch Battalion; and the suburbs on the right, which had given us so much trouble, were this day evacuated by the enemy.

During the 17th and 18th our advance was pushed still further, the line of the streets being avoided whenever the resistance was determined, and the houses on both sides being sapped through instead. It was not till the 19th, however, that we were able to seize the Burn Bastion, commanding the Lahore Gate, and thus obtained possession of the Chandee

* I am indebted to Major Norman's Narrative for the doings of the army from the 15th to the 20th. But I shall make no apology to "Felix," for occasionally quoting his letter, published in the above Narrative.

Chouk. Meanwhile, our constant shelling had produced its effect. The resistance to our advance was growing feebler every day, and the enemy's line of retreat being open, he escaped in great numbers from the gates on the south side of the town. The palace being apparently evacuated, the gate was blown open with powder, and the place occupied, with scarcely any opposition, some thirty rebels being slain inside.

On the 20th the whole place was in our hands; and on the 21st, Captain Hodson, with a party of his horse, captured the fugitive King in the bold manner which has so often been recorded in the public papers.

Thus ended the Siege of Delhi, after nearly four months of continual fighting, of harassing work, and of constant exposure, during the most sickly season of the year. The handful of troops, that had so manfully held their ground for so long, were at length able to assume the offensive, and, after one of the most desperate and sanguinary sieges on record, obtained possession of a strongly fortified city, containing 200 guns and an immense supply of ammunition, from a garrison more than treble their own numbers.

One thousand six hundred and seventy men and officers, killed and wounded, fell in the actual siege, from the 7th to the 20th of September, of which (as has been said above) 1,170 fell on the great day of the assault. The total loss of the army, from June to September, was 3,837 men, killed, wounded, and missing,—besides very many more, who died of their wounds, or of disease and exposure, of whom I have no account,—out of a force never numbering 10,000 effectives.

No army ever deserved better of their country.

The political and military results of the success were incalculable; as, though we know the good it produced, we shall never know the evil it prevented.

It was the first great blow struck at the rebel cause, and from that time the tide of battle has steadily flowed in our favour.

It secured the Punjab, then beginning to waver; it saved Agra, and re-conquered the N.W. Provinces; and it gave a powerful reinforcement to the Commander-in-Chief, which enabled him finally to extricate the garrison of Lucknow.

Our camp had been moved forward to the Metcalfe Park on the 18th, so as to be nearer the work. The wounded, however, were left in the old camp till the 23rd, when all that could be moved went into the city, and were established at Deriougunge, where the Engineer head-quarters had been fixed.

As soon as I was strong enough, I paid several visits to different parts of the city, with an account of which I need not fatigue the reader, as Delhi has been so often described. The great magazine was full of guns, shot, and shells, as if the siege was just about to begin; and, in illustration of the rumours so often spread, that the besieged were running short of percussion caps, I may mention that we found 600,000 in the expense magazine of one bastion alone. In a corner of the court-yard of the great magazine were the ruins of the place where the small-arm ammunition was kept, and which was the building blown up by poor Willoughby, who thus deprived the rebels of the use of six millions of ball cartridges.

The aspect of the city was most ruinous and desolate; not that the houses had suffered much by our shot, for our fire had been of necessity almost entirely directed against the fortifications, but nearly the whole of the inhabitants had fled, and the houses were all completely gutted.

Head-quarters were at first established in Skinner's House, afterwards in the Dewan Khass in the palace.

All the strong points of the city, including the gateways, were held by our guards. The Rifles and Goorkhas garrisoned the palace. I paid a visit to the Jumma Musjid, then occupied by Coke's Rifles. It is a noble structure, built of great blocks of red sandstone, ornamented with white marble, and distinguished by a grand massiveness of design not often found in Oriental architecture, which usually deals more in elaborate ornament and very minute finish.

The army was so totally exhausted by the exertions it had been called upon to make, that it was not for several days after we had final possession of the city that two columns, under Brigadiers Greathed and Showers, were despatched in pursuit of the flying enemy.

The operations of the latter were confined to the neigbouring districts. The former, it is well known, after relieving Agra, swept down the Grand Trunk Road, and, joining the Commander-in-Chief at Cawnpore, took part in the final relief of Lucknow. Only two Engineers and a small detachment of Sappers were sent with this column, whose operations were at first intended to be far less extensive.

The head-quarters of the Engineer Brigade were detained at Delhi, and, finding there was no immediate prospect of active service, I applied for and obtained a short leave to the hills, and, on the 29th, in company with two others, started for Mussooree.

We travelled by palkee gharee, and accomplished our journey of 150 miles without any molestation. It was a curious proof of our prestige, that, only nine days after the termination of such a contest, three people could travel along the high roads in such perfect security.

We passed the ruins of many a village that had been burnt by us, for harbouring rebels; or by the Goojurs, to avenge some private quarrel. All our police chokees were destroyed, but the bridges everywhere were unhurt, the enemy having found them too useful to blow up.

We crossed the suspension bridge over the Hindun, and saw the site of the first battle in which our troops had encountered the rebels, in May last, when General Wilson's column was on its way from Meerut to Delhi.

At Meerut we saw the formidable fortifications made by our Engineers to protect the station, and paid a visit to the blackened and burnt lines of the two Native Regiments where the mutiny first broke out.

From Meerut we went, *viâ* Mozuffernuggur, to Roorkee, passing up the Ganges canal bank for some ten miles of its course. The locks had been injured, and many chokees were burnt; but the head-works having always remained in our hands, little injury had been done on the whole, thanks to the gallant little garrison of Roorkee. The water had just been let in at the head, and we met it flowing down as we passed up. At Roorkee I visited, for the first time, the canal workshops, steam saw mills, &c., and admired, as every Engineer must, that monument of scientific skill, the Solani Aqueduct.

The following morning found us through the Mohun Pass, in the Sewalik Hills, and driving across the beautiful valley of the Dhoon, to the foot of the Himalayahs. A steep ascent of 6,000 feet, in a length of eight miles, took us to the fresh mountain air and grand scenery of Mussooree.

Here I stayed two months, the change being indeed delightful, from the heat, the turmoil, and the numerous disagreeables of camp, to the cool breezes, the quietude, and the social charms of Mussooree. In this favoured spot, as at the other hill stations, great numbers of ladies and children had remained in security during the past struggle; not without alarms, indeed, but still safe from the anxieties and dangers that so many of the gentler sex had encountered in the stations in the plains.

Many sick and wounded officers were already up, and numbers continued to arrive daily. There was, however, very little gaiety. It was sad, during church time, to observe the large number of ladies in the deepest mourning, telling that they had been amongst those who had lost near and dear relatives by death in battle, sickness in camp, or by massacre at the hands of the rebels.

Now, however, that all felt the turning point in the struggle was past, bright eyes looked once more cheerful, and pale faces began again to resume their natural hues. We heard day after day the glad news of the first relief of Lucknow; of the approach of the Commander-in-Chief, with reinforcements, to Cawnpore; of the defeat of the rebels, under the walls of Agra, by the Delhi column; of the triumphal march of Greathed's little force to Cawnpore; of their junction with the Commander-in-Chief; of the march on Lucknow, and terrific slaughter of the rebels at the Secundra Bagh; and finally, of the successful withdrawal of the Lucknow garrison.

I expected daily to hear of the Engineer Brigade moving down towards Oude, and was prepared at once to join them; but they got to Agra, and could get no further. The road thence to Cawnpore was completely in the hands of the rebels: our small party of Sappers could not have forced their way down, and for some time there were no troops to spare to furnish any more reinforcements.

I stayed the whole of my leave at Mussooree until the 26th November, and then turned my steps once more to the Engineer camp.

CHAPTER X.

FROM MUSSOOREE TO AGRA.

I LEFT Mussooree at the end of November, and travelling back to Meerut, quitted that place by the passenger van for Agra, with five or six other travellers: the road was perfectly quiet; but our police stations and Dák Bungalows had been burnt by the rebels. We passed by Bolundshahur, where Greathed's column had thrashed the rebels, and through the city of Allyghur, where he had beaten them again; the fort, however lies some distance off the road, so I could not then visit it. We arrived at Agra the same evening, and crossing the bridge of boats, drove straight to cantonments, where I found the Engineer Brigade encamped, and had the pleasure of meeting my old Delhi friends.

The reader probably knows that Agra lies on the Jumna, 120 miles below Delhi, and on the same side of the river. The fort lies close to the city, but does not form part of it, and the city itself is not fortified in any way like Delhi. The cantonments and civil lines are, as usual, some distance off. The importance of this large and strong fort was incalculable during the mutiny. The Europeans, from Neemuch, Nusserabad, Allyghur, Muttra, and numerous other stations, civil and military, here found a refuge; and being the capital of the N.W. Provinces, the political importance of our possession of it could hardly be overrated.

But, for a long time, every one was shut up inside the fort walls, and nothing could be called our own that was out of the range of our guns. All regular communication with the surrounding country was cut off; and it was only by *kossids* that the garrison received or sent any news.

The Gwalior Contingent were advancing to besiege it, not having heard the news of the fall of Delhi, when they were defeated by Greathed's column close to the very walls, on the 10th of October. From that time the intercourse with Delhi and the Punjab, and with Bombay, by a somewhat circuitous route, was tolerably safe and uninterrupted. But though the Delhi column had forced its way down to Cawnpore, it could not keep the road open, and the communication from Agra downwards was still vague and precarious; the regular post coming round by Bombay.

The first had been garrisoned all along by the 3rd Europeans, which had done very good service, besides, in sending out detachments to thrash the rebels in the neighbourhood, at Hattrass, and elsewhere. When I arrived, the fort was crowded with men, women, and children: a census, taken a short time before, giving 7,000 people as the number then inhabiting the place.

The Engineer Brigade had been marched to Agra, with a view to their proceeding down country to join the Commander-in-Chief, but the Chief Commissioner at Agra refused to let them proceed any further, as I have already mentioned; and for the last six weeks the Sappers had been marching about the neighbouring districts with detachments of the 3rd Europeans, or the native police, collecting revenue, or punishing refractory villages.

The day after my arrival I called on some old friends in the fort, and in the evening went to visit the celebrated Taj. It has been so often described, that I need not trouble the reader with a lengthened account of it. I was disappointed, as most people are, on the first view of it. The domes appeared to me inelegant, and the dead mass of white building seemed to require some relief. The minarets, however, struck me as being the most exquisitely graceful things of the kind I had ever seen; and the general effect of the whole building, as it stands out from the foliage of the dark cypress, trees is undoubtedly beautiful and imposing. A large convoy of hackeries, camels, and commissariat stores was collected at Agra, and a still larger one at Delhi, both waiting to proceed down country. Colonel Seaton, with a small force of cavalry, infantry, and guns, was to escort them down to join the Commander-in-Chief, who was in urgent want of these stores.

The Chief had just relieved Lucknow, and having left General Outram with 4,500 men at Alumbagh, was about to advance up country.

A portion of the Sappers was, at this time, ordered to take some guns and ammunition to the fort at Allyghur; and Captain Taylor, the Commanding Engineer, obtained permission for the head-quarters of the Brigade to proceed with it, as it was the best chance of our getting down to the Chief.

On the 8th of December we accordingly left Agra for Allyghur, with the head-quarters of the Engineer Brigade and the Muzbee Sappers; the Bengal Sappers remaining behind.

On the 10th we reached Allyghur, having accomplished a forced march of thirty-five miles that day, as we received an express to hurry on lest we should be attacked. The threatened attack, we found out afterwards, was a myth, and the forced march was unnecessary; however, it gave us two days' halt at Allyghur, before Seaton's column joined from Delhi.

We encamped close to the fort, and the next morning paid a visit to the place.

The work is an old native one, which was improved on European principles, by some of the French Engineers, who were formerly in the Mahratta service. It has a massive rampart, with a wide and deep wet ditch all round, and two ravelins at the entrances.

It was now garrisoned by three companies of the 3rd Europeans, and a company of Seikhs and some artillerymen. The town, which is a good-sized one, is about two miles off. The small civil and military station lay between the two, and had, like all others, been plundered by the mutineers.

Allygurh is on the Grand Trunk Road, at the point where the Meerut and Agra road crosses it, and it is therefore a post of considerable importance. The fort was now being repaired, and temporary barracks being built for the accommodation of the garrison.

Seaton's column arrived on the 11th, bringing in the immense convoy from Delhi. It consisted of several thousands of hackeries and camels, and stretched for twelve miles along the road in one continuous line.

Of course it was impossible to guard such an immense convoy with a few men, and it was now to remain at Allyghur, until the column should have cleared the road of the rebels, and be able to form a junction with the Commander-in-Chief; the immense number of animals and carts was, therefore, located outside the fort, under the protection of its guns; and Seaton's force, which we now joined, prepared to move on.

This force consisted of the 1st Bengal Fusileers; 7th Punjab Infantry; 1 squadron of Carbineers; Hodson's Horse; 2 heavy guns; Bishop's troop of Horse Artillery; and three companies of Punjab Sappers, forming a total perhaps of 2,500 fighting men. It was, in the first instance, to proceed towards Khasgunge, in the direction of Futtyghur, where the rebels were known to be in force, and had had undisturbed possession of the country for the last four months. If these could be dispersed, the march of the convoy would be tolerably safe, as far as Mynpoorie, where intelligence would probably be obtained of the movements of the Commander-in-Chief.

CHAPTER XI.

SEATON'S CAMPAIGN IN THE DOAB.

On the 12th December, I left Allyghur with Seaton's column. The bugle sounded at 2 a.m., and by 3 we were marching down the Grand Trunk Road. After proceeding along it for six miles, we turned off to the left, and took the district kucha road to Khasgunge. Videttes of cavalry were thrown out for some distance on both flanks, and the advanced guard consisted of a troop of cavalry, two guns, and three companies of infantry, and Sappers. We crossed the Ganges Canal by a fine masonry bridge, and proceeded over a well-cultivated country, till we reached our first halting ground at Jullailee, twelve miles from Allyghur. Here we remained encamped for the day without any adventure, and the next morning marched to Gungeree, about twelve miles further on.

This marching work is pleasant enough in cold weather, except for the very early hour at which it is necessary to rise, so as to secure the march being over and the tents pitched before the day has begun to grow hot. However, one gets used, in time, even to getting up at 1 a.m. The weather was intensely cold, and after dressing in the dark, and drinking a cup of coffee by one of the huge camp fires, I was glad enough when the column got into motion to walk some three or four miles for the sake of the warmth. About sunrise, the halt was usually sounded for half an hour. The men got their grog, and officers dismounted and discussed sandwiches and biscuits, with a nip of raw brandy or whiskey, which put a little life into one's chilled veins. Then the advance sounded, and the column once more moved on, and arrived at its camping ground at seven or eight o'clock. Then the quarter-masters having marked out the ground for the several regiments, the men sat down to rest there till the tents came up, and soon a little town of canvas would rise up in the former bare plain.

Officers sat down under the trees until their tents should be pitched, and the breakfast, which was brought on in doolies or on mules, or by horse and cart, being quickly spread in the shade, we used to enjoy our picnic amazingly, and, reclining on the grass with pipes in mouths, felt a happy indifference to the chances of meeting any indefinite number of Pandies that fate might ordain. By the time we had smoked our pipes, the tents were ready, every one retired to his canvas home, and in reading, writing, or sleeping, to make up for his short night's rest, the day usually passed. In the evening, we again met for dinner, and turned in very soon afterwards, most of us being sound asleep by eight o'clock, to be woke up again at one for the next day's march.

Having arrived at Gungeree on our second day's march, we pitched our camp as usual, and discussed the probabilities of the enemy making a stand at Khasgunge the next day. Most of us thought he would not; and, having eaten our breakfast as usual, I was about to lie down for a nap, when I heard a row in camp—a sound of distant firing—and, running out of my tent, discovered to my astonishment that the troops were getting under arms, and falling in, in front of their lines. So I mounted, and rode forward, and found the enemy were right on us, and, having driven in our advanced picket, communicated the intelligence of their arrival by sending three or four round shot into camp.

They seemed to have a perfect swarm of cavalry, not many guns, and a good number of infantry, but it was not very easy to make out their exact force; the ground was flat and even, but a good deal of it consisted of tall Bajera fields, which might have concealed any number.

It appeared afterwards that they were about 5,000 strong, and were quite unaware of our proximity. There was a small detachment in the district—some

250 men of the Belooch Battalion, with a couple of guns, and the rebels had determined to attack them—so they left Khasgunge the previous night, and in the morning came upon our camp, and, concluding it was the small force they had come to attack, advanced very boldly. They were soon undeceived.

To their horror out dashed eight Horse Artillery guns at the gallop, and commenced firing into them at cruelly close quarters; while a strong body of cavalry advancing to the support of the guns, and our long line of infantry drawn up in front of the camp, showed them what a terrible mistake they had made. It is true they were about three to one, but Pandy will not fight in the open at such short odds as these; and they were quite willing to take to their heels, if we would have let them go away in peace: in fact, a great part of them began to make off at once, but it was too late.

Our guns were pouring round shot and grape into them, and Hodson's Horse, cutting them off from an attempt to get round our left, charged right into them. At the same time, the Carbineers rode at the guns, which Pandy was making desperate efforts to get away in his flight. Seeing he was too late, he very pluckily stuck to them, sending a shell right into the squadron, which killed an officer, and knocked over several men. The next moment the gunners were sabred and the guns our own, and then the cavalry rode amongst the flying and scattered infantry, and sabred them in hundreds; many of them, however, fought desperately, and we lost forty men killed and wounded in the cavalry alone, including three officers of the Carbineers.

The flying enemy were pursued nearly five miles, and then our artillery and cavalry returned to camp. The infantry had advanced in readiness for action, but were not called upon to fire a shot.

I was with the staff all the time, and the whole affair was more like a field day at a review than a battle. As we rode back through the fields, many wounded wretches were found hiding in the fields, and were shot or cut down without mercy. Several rebels had taken refuge in the trees, and were shot there. The ground all round was in fact strewed with dead bodies, and at least 300 were killed.

The camp was again quiet by 3 p.m., but a gloom was thrown over the day's success by the loss of three officers in one single squadron of Carbineers, the fourth, moreover, being severely wounded. The next morning we marched to Khasgunge; the troops were ordered to take cooked rations with them, as it was thought the enemy would make a stand at that place, which was a good-sized town, and had long been their head-quarters in this part of the country.

However, the advanced guard of cavalry, pushing on under Captain Hodson, found the town evacuated by the rebels. But many of the inhabitants remained, and seemed really glad to welcome us, calling out that now they should no longer be oppressed and plundered.

As we entered the town, we found the dead body of a man hanging up by the heels to a tree; he had been one of our Native spies, and the rebels, having caught him, had hung him up head downwards, and then stabbed him to death. The sight did not tend to soften our feelings towards the brutes, most of whom we knew were a mere rabble of low caste Mussulmans, raised by the Nawab of Furruckabad and his followers.

We encamped at Khasgunge, in a pretty tope of trees, and next morning pushed on for Suhawun, the rebels still retreating as we advanced. Several of their stragglers were found in the villages we passed, and were instantly shot; and Hodson, with the advanced guard, caught the tail of their column at Suhawun, and cut up some thirty of them.

That day searching parties were ordered into the village, and nearly 100 rebels were found concealed, and summarily shot or hanged; and then the village, being plundered of everything, was fired, as it was a notorious nest of *budmashes*.

The following day we resumed our pursuit of the retreating enemy. We knew that they had guns and carts with them, and heard that their bullocks were getting tired, so that they must either fight or abandon them.

From the villagers we learned that they really intended standing at Puttialee, and to that place we marched accordingly. We were within two miles of the place, and I was riding with the advanced guard, when through the morning mist, which had not yet disappeared, we saw a strong picket of the enemy's cavalry within 300 yards of us. They fell back so slowly and deliberately that the advanced guard closed up to charge them, but they did not give us an opportunity, retreating rapidly on the village. From that place we now heard a confused hum of voices, which showed that there was a large body of the enemy there collected; and soon a couple of round shot flying towards us made us no longer doubt that the force we had been pursuing had resolved at length to fight, having been reinforced probably by others from Furruckabad.

The two guns of the advanced guard were now halted on the road, and the cavalry spread to the right and left to watch the enemy. Meanwhile, word had been sent back to Colonel Seaton, who was with the main column, and this was now brought up and halted, until a reconnaissance should be made of the enemy's position.

The advanced cavalry then pushed on slowly until we were within long range of the enemy's guns, which were immediately opened upon us, and discovered to us their position and number. I rode forward with Captain T—— to examine the enemy's right, and Captain Hodson, and G——, of the Engineers, were also busy on the other side. The enemy had posted himself in front of the village, his right resting on a ravine or nullah, his centre crossing the road, and partially defended by slight intrenchments; his left quite open, and apparently depending for protection on the mass of cavalry there posted. Two or three of the guns were put to rake the road; the remainder (there were fourteen in all) were distributed here and there along the front. They were as busy as bees in strengthening their field works, and resented our impudence in advancing to look at them by sending several shot at us, one of which we watched as it spent itself, picked it up, and found it to be only a 3-pounder, so we carried it back to show to the Colonel.

It was evident that the left of the enemy was the proper point of attack, and our infantry, diverging from the road, were drawn up in some fields on the right, and were formed into line. As soon as all was ready, four guns of the Horse Artillery went to the front at the gallop, supported by part of the Carbineers, and opened with shell on the enemy's cavalry. These never attempted to stand, but in an instant scampered off as fast as their horses' legs could carry them; then the guns, again advancing, took up a position so as to rake the whole of the enemy's line from the right, while two guns, that had been sent down the road, played away on the left. He could not stand the raking fire long: he had expected we should attack him in front, running our heads against his guns and earthworks, and was taken aback by his flank being turned in this way. After a feeble attempt to reply to our fire, he fled, and the artillery and cavalry, charging down on his camp, took possession of it. Fourteen guns, several carts and limbers, full of ammunition, tents, &c., were all taken, and the routed enemy was hotly pursued down the road and across the country. The infantry, coming up, skirmished through the fields and grass jungle, and shot down many who were wounded, or had taken refuge in trees. For seven miles the routed rebels were chased by the cavalry, and fell, sabred in hundreds. I went on with the pursuit that day, and never saw such a scene. The men attempted no resistance; they threw away their arms, and submitted patiently to the death stroke. Six hundred of them fell, and we lost but one man killed and one wounded. One could hardly help feeling pity for these misguided wretches (very few of whom were Sepoys), who had left their peaceful occupations to fight no better than this. But we all knew that the retribution was just and necessary, and that not a particle of mercy would have been shown by them to any one that might fall into their hands. Their valiant commander (I forget his name) fled away on an elephant before a shot was fired; but finding the pursuit too hot, got on his horse, and unfortunately escaped. I asked one of our native officers how it was, if these people could not make a better stand than this, they did not run away beforehand like sensible men? He said, "Sir, they are ignorant wretches, and know nothing. Their head men tell them lies about the English, incite them to fight, assure them of victory, and promise that they will stand by them to the last; but as soon as the chiefs hear the sound of a gun, their livers become water; they run away with their cavalry, and leave the poor devils of infantry to their fate." As we went over the field of battle, one of us found a wounded rebel Sepoy, and asked what regiment he belonged to, and various questions about the force that he had been with. He answered all the questions, and then said, "Now, sir, that I have told you everything, have the kindness to have me taken into hospital." This will give some idea of one of the many phases of the Sepoy character. Here was a scoundrel taken in arms against the Government he served, who would have put to death, in cold blood, any European who fell into his hands, and who, very probably, had lent a hand in some of the massacres that had taken place, and who now fully expected to be taken into hospital, cured of his wound, and allowed to go free! Many other similar cases occurred. When the Sappers mutinied at Meerut, shot their commanding officer, and were pursued and cut up by the Carbineers and Horse Artillery, more than one wounded man fled to Roorkee, the head-quarters of his corps, walked deliberately into the hospital, and asked to have his wounds dressed, without attempting to conceal how he had received them. There was a general idea throughout the country that however badly they might behave, nothing would induce us to resort to extreme severity; and I have no doubt that numbers joined the rebel cause for the sake of plunder and the *tumasha* (fun), and thinking that the utmost punishment that ever could overtake them would be to be tried in a regular court, after the orthodox fashion, and with a very good chance of escape.

The King of Delhi's sons, when captured by Hodson, said, with a jaunty air, "Of course there will be a proper investigation into our conduct in the proper court."

And this feeling, however creditable to the moderation of our rule, shows the mischief caused by attempting to rule such a people in such a way. We must rule Asiatics with a rod of iron, or they cannot be ruled at all; and, as European rulers, we should treat them as children, so far as to insist upon their doing what we know to be best for them, and never give way to them in any single instance.

Enough, however, of this digression. We remained at Puttialee for three days. We were now within four or five marches of Futtyghur, the great stronghold of the rebels in the Doab, and I have little doubt that if we could have pushed on at once, such was the consternation throughout the country, that we could have taken the place even with our small force. But Colonel Seaton's first object was to get the convoy safe down to the Commander-in-Chief, who could hardly move for want of it; and, moreover, there was a strong force of rebels on the other side of the river, who were threatening to cross, and might have disturbed the whole district again in our rear; so it was determined to retrace our steps to Gungeree, to enable us to cross the Kala Nuddie, and then, striking the Grand Trunk Road at Etah, push on to Mynpoorie, and get the convoy down so far. We accordingly marched back as we had come, and arrived at Gungeree once more, without any more fighting. On the road, Hodson got information of a rebel leader being concealed in a village a short distance off, and surrounding it suddenly, seized the man. He had been a Native officer in the 3rd Irregular Cavalry, and had retired on a handsome pension. He had been very active in the rebel cause; two of his sons had been killed fighting against us, and the third was still in arms in the district. All this having been proved before the Military Commission sitting in camp, he was sentenced to be blown from the mouth of a cannon that afternoon.

At 4 p.m. a portion of the troops, ordered to form a parade, drew up in three sides of a hollow square, with the gun in the centre, facing the fourth or open side; the prisoner was marched in between two sentries, and the charge and sentence read aloud in English and Hindostanee. He was very pale, but perfectly calm; held himself upright, and seemed resolved to die like a soldier. He must have been nearly sixty, but did not look so old, as his beard was dyed. He marched firmly up to the gun, a 6-pounder, which was already loaded with a blank charge; his back was placed on the muzzle, and his arms tied to the two wheels. Directly this was done, the Artillery officer made a signal, the gun was fired, and the wretched man had ceased to exist. The troops were marched in front of the gun to look at the body, and the parade broke off. The body was blown clean in two, the legs and stomach falling close to the gun, the head and chest being thrown forward some three or four yards, and the arms torn from the body, and lying on the ground. It was a horrible sight; but a more painless death could hardly be devised.

On arriving at Gungeree, I received an order from the Major-General commanding the division to repair to Delhi, as I had been appointed Garrison Engineer there. I was not particularly pleased, as I was hoping to get down country to join the grand army, and thought I should be shut out of all the operations at Lucknow; however, "to hear was to obey," and bidding adieu to my Engineer friends, I marched back to Allyghur, with the detachment escorting the captured guns and wounded men from the column.

At Allyghur I remained some days, to allow my servants and traps to go on before, and then, taking a seat in the passenger van, reached Delhi on the 1st January, 1858.

Seaton's column marched to Mynporie, defeating the rebel Rajah there with great slaughter, and the road being thus clear, the huge convoys from Allyghur and Agra marched down country. The Commander-in-Chief had meanwhile started from Cawnpore to come up to Futtyghur; and the junction between the two forces being effected, the Grand Trunk Road from Cawnpore to Delhi was once more open for travellers and mail carts, after the communication had been closed for nearly six months.

The whole of this little campaign was well managed, was highly successful, and of the greatest service in quieting the country; and Colonel Seaton, who had before served with distinction in Affghanistan, and had been wounded at Delhi, was deservedly made a Brigadier and K.C.B.

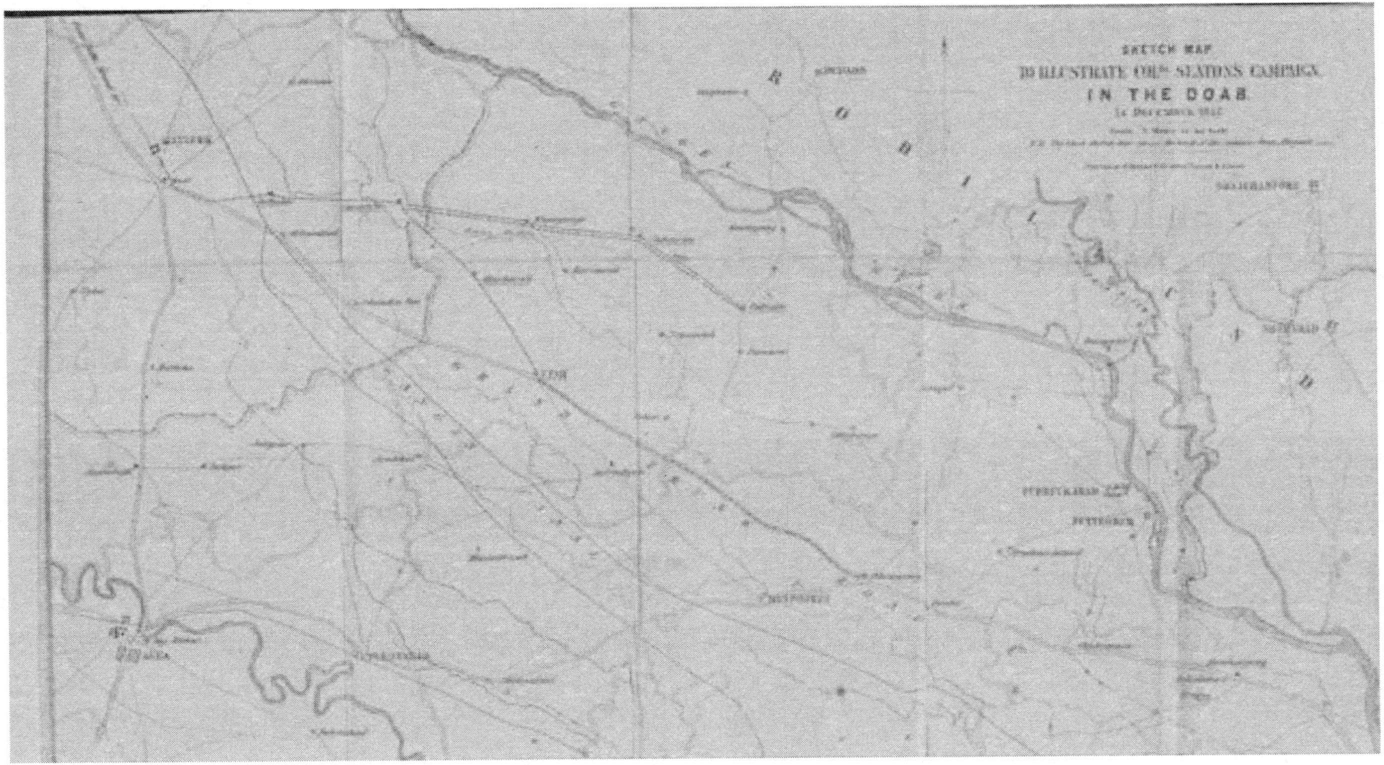
SKETCH MAP
IN THE DOAB

CHAPTER XII.

FROM DELHI TO ALUMBAGH.

I FOUND Delhi as quiet and peaceable as if no such thing as a siege had ever occurred. The breaches were mended, our old batteries levelled, and only here and there some traces to be found of the great struggle. The ruined cantonments were, however, completely deserted, all the troops being quartered in the city and palace. Ladies had joined their husbands; the inhabitants had returned to the city; and the place looked once more populous and lively. I had work to do in providing accommodation for the troops, but it was not yet settled what was to be done with the fortifications. They were at first ordered to be destroyed, but the order was subsequently countermanded; and I ventured to suggest that they might be retained, and manned by a small garrison, by turning the bastions into isolated forts capable of firing on the town, as well as on an enemy outside. Nothing, however, was done while I was there, and I do not know what course has since been determined on.

Towards the end of the month I obtained a few days' leave to visit Mussooree on private affairs, and found that usually gay place, now that the season was past, silent and deserted, the hills covered with snow—a sight to gladden the eyes of any one who had been nine years in the plains of India. I went down in a few days to Umballa, and was then ordered to return to my civil appointment in the Punjab, when the same day brought me a telegraphic message to proceed and join the Engineer Brigade once more, now before Lucknow. I started off the same night (the 11th of February).

The Commander-in-Chief, having taken Futtyghur, the last stronghold of the rebels in the Doab, had remained there for some time, waiting for the siege train, and supplies of ammunition from the Agra and Delhi magazines. As soon as these were received, he returned to Cawnpore, where the grand army was now assembled for the attack on Lucknow.

The army had already in a great part crossed the Ganges into Oude, and it was stated that the attack was to be made at once. So I travelled day and night, and reached Cawnpore on the 15th, without molestation, though the road was not over and above safe, as a brother of the Nana's, and some 500 of his adherents, were crossing over to get to Calpee.

On my way down, I passed my old friends of the

2nd Punjab Cavalry, who were marching on in hot haste from the Punjab, very anxious lest they should not be in time for the grand drama. At Meerun-Ka-Serai, fifty miles above Cawnpore, I found the 7th Punjab Infantry employed in watching the Ghats near at hand, so as to prevent the escape of the enemy from Oude. Twenty miles further on I found Walpole's Brigade encamped, and met some old friends in the 2nd Punjab Infantry; they had been ordered out from Cawnpore, in hopes of intercepting the Nana, or his brother, who, as above remarked, were trying to cross the Doab.

I reached Cawnpore late in the evening, and met a hearty welcome from S——, the executive Engineer, at whose house I found quite a party of Engineers assembled, including two Royal Engineer officers, who, like myself, were bound for Lucknow. One of these, who was afterwards killed, I had known at Chatham ten years before.

I found that the Commander-in-Chief and all his staff were still at Cawnpore, and that there was no immediate intention of an advance on Lucknow. Sir J. Outram was still at Alumbagh, where he had been ever since our evacuation of the Residency; and the Engineer camp was pitched close to his, where the brigade was busily engaged in preparing materials for the siege.

It was reported that very severe work lay before us. The rebels were said to be 80,000 strong, and to have fortified the city with a series of earthworks *à la* Sebastopol, of immense strength and solidity. Pandy's courage had been raised by our forced evacuation of the city in November last; and if he did not fight now, at his own head-quarters, and to defend his own country, he was not likely to fight at all.

The army, 20,000 strong, with 180 guns, had nearly all crossed the river, and was on the road between Cawnpore and Lucknow, stationed in various camps, all ready to advance when they got the word. No one knew when the attack was to come off, but the Chief was said to be waiting for the convoy of women and children to pass down to Allahabad, and also for the junction of the columns of General Franks and Jung Bahadoor, which were advancing upwards from the Gorruckpore direction.

The journey between Cawnpore and Alumbagh (forty-five miles) would have to be done on horseback. I arranged to proceed with the two Royal Engineers; and the 16th was employed in procuring camels, and in making sundry purchases and preparations for the journey. My servants and horses were all behind, coming along the road by double marches, but could not be down for a fortnight, at least. With some difficulty, however, I procured two men that would answer my purpose temporarily; and then I went over to an itinerant horse dealer's, to try and procure a steed; but being asked 350 rupees for a marvellously ill-favoured quadruped, that would have been dear in the Punjab at 100 rupees, I gave up the attempt in despair, and through the kindness of G——, of my corps, who had left his railway appointment once more to join the army, was promised a mount from his stud.

The day was hot and abominably dusty—as Cawnpore always is,—and the whole place looked so dreary and wretched, with its burnt bungalows and barracks, that I had no fancy for strolling about in the sun, even to see poor General Wheeler's famous intrenchment.

I walked over to the hotel in the evening, and found it full of officers, who, from the great difficulties of conversation between them and their servants, were evidently new arrivals. The price of every article (including the wages of servants) was enormously increased by the immense importation of British officers and men, who, of course, knowing nothing of the language or the ways and habits of the people, were fleeced inordinately by their domestics. Many of the officers, indeed, endured serious discomfort at first, from the impossibility of procuring servants; having to cook their own food as they best might, and being unable to procure such common necessaries of clothing as boots, shoes, &c. Things, however, were much better now, as the demand had soon created a tolerable supply, and the Governments of the N.W. Provinces and Punjab had sent down with the convoys many of the above necessaries for the use of the troops.

On the morning of the 17th we left Cawnpore, and, crossing one of the two bridges of boats that were lying under the guns of our entrenchment, cantered on to Oonao, nine miles distant, the scene of one of Havelock's battles, and now occupied by one of our large camps.

I found the Highland Brigade assembled here; and very pleasant it was to see the stalwart figures in their kilts and tartans, even if it was accompanied by the penalty of hearing the bagpipes. My old Derajat and Delhi friends, the 4th Punjab Rifles, were brigaded with the Highlanders, and I put up for the day with their Commanding Officer. This regiment, as well as the 2nd Punjab Infantry, had come down with Greathed's column, and had done splendid service, charging into the Secundra Bagh, at the memorable struggle there, shoulder to shoulder with the Highlanders.

The Punjabees were on capital terms with the soldiers

of the 93rd, the two corps fraternizing together most harmoniously. Indeed, the men from the hills, hearing that these were *our* hill soldiers, looked upon them as brothers, and took a great delight in the skirl of the pipes. The 2nd and 4th Punjab Infantry, and Brasyer's Regiment of Seikhs, were the only regiments of Native Infantry in camp, and were worked off their legs till the end of the campaign. Some thirty men and officers of Wilde's corps had the red ribbon of the Order of Merit for the Secundra Bagh and other fights, and were evidently very proud of it. It is a great pity that this admirable Order is not extended to the European army: while the French have the Legion of Honour, the Military Medal, and, I believe, one or two others, the only decoration that the officers and soldiers of the English army, from the grade of Captain downwards, can hope to get, is the Victoria Cross, which is, and ought to be, only given in very rare and exceptional cases; and, after all, only rewards one quality (valour) out of the many which are requisite to make a good soldier, such as intelligence, knowledge of his duty, steadiness, obedience, &c.

We dined and slept at Oonao, and the following evening rode on to Nuwabgunge, sixteen miles further, with an escort carrying stores to the front. Here we found another camp, and I had the pleasure of meeting the only European Infantry Corps that had served at Delhi, and was now going to help to take Lucknow,—I mean the 1st European Bengal Fusileers, one of the finest regiments in the service, which had come down with Seaton's column.

I dined at their mess that night, and next day went on to Bunnee, where we found the 79th Highlanders and a Madras regiment encamped. Introducing ourselves to the officers of the former, they very kindly gave us some breakfast; and, as we found an escort had just gone on to Alumbagh, from which we were now only ten miles distant, we rode on directly after breakfast, in hopes of overtaking them. We saw nothing of them, however, but were unmolested on our journey by any stray Pandies; and, about 1 p.m., found ourselves in the middle of Sir J. Outram's celebrated camp at Alumbagh, which he had held for three months with a small force, encamped in the open, against the whole rebel power of Lucknow, or rather of the Province of Oude. The troops were partly hutted, and had evidently made themselves very comfortable. The Alumbagh lay in front of the camp, the house and garden being held by a detachment; and a few sullen reports, and puffs of white smoke in the distance, told that the same sort of daily exchange of shots was going on here to which one had been so accustomed at Delhi.

I found that the Engineers' camp was pitched about a mile to the right, close to the fort of Jellalabad; and, riding across the intervening plain, I had the gratification of once more shaking hands with most of my old Delhi friends, and of being introduced to a large number of new faces, principally among our brethren of the Royal Engineers.

The Chief Engineer, Brigadier Napier, was still with the Commander-in-Chief at Cawnpore, and Colonel H——, of the Royal Engineers, was now temporarily in command of the brigade. We had a very large number of officers, including twelve Royal Engineers, and several Line officers, who had been serving as field Engineers in the Residency.

In addition to the Bengal Sappers, the Punjab Sappers, and the Delhi Pioneers, who had all been at Delhi, we had two companies of Royal Engineers, and a company of the Madras Sappers: so that the brigade numbered some 3,000 men and 60 officers; and, as we all messed together, we had by far the largest mess in camp.

CHAPTER XIII.

ALUMBAGH IN FEBRUARY, 1858.

Sir J. Outram's camp at Alumbagh was about a mile in rear of the Alumbagh itself, which was a large walled garden, with a house inside, situated on the Cawnpore road, about two miles from the outskirts of Lucknow. In this enclosure the baggage of Outram and Havelock's force was left, under a guard, when they went in to relieve the Residency; but being unable to do more than join the beleaguered garrison, the Alumbagh post was closely invested by the enemy during the two months that elapsed, until the second relief was achieved by the Commander-in-Chief. When Sir Colin returned to Cawnpore, after extricating the garrison, Sir J. Outram was left, as above observed, with 4,500 men at Alumbagh, partly to threaten the city, and so to keep the rebels there *en masse*, and partly to prevent any bad moral effect which might have arisen had we entirely relinquished Oude at this juncture.

Outram's camp was pitched in the open, a strong picket being established at Alumbagh, and the camp itself being defended by batteries, abattis, &c., and by judiciously turning two or three swamps to account, which, however, in February were pretty nearly dry.

Skirmishing went on all day long between our advanced pickets and those of the enemy, and his distant batteries usually blazed away a little, morning and evening, but without doing very much damage. On certain days, Pandy would screw up his courage to make an attack, and then out they swarmed, very much in the old Delhi fashion; clouds of men advancing in front and on both flanks, and coming on very valiantly, until they got within grape distance of our guns, when they were usually pounded by the artillery, and, if they gave a chance, charged by the cavalry. Olphert's Battery and the Military Train particularly distinguished themselves in this work, and many hundreds of Pandies were slain in these attacks by these two corps.

We had a Sapper picket in the fort of Jellalabad, which was on the extreme right of the position, and in this fort was part of our park, the rest being in rear of our camp. The Engineers were now busily employed in the preparation of gabions, fascines, and other siege materiel, and in the construction of a cask-bridge, to cross part of the force over the Goomtee, for the operations on the left bank of that river. I was employed, after a time, in experimenting on the best and quickest way of blowing down walls, doors, &c., with bags of powder; and by the end of the month we were quite ready to begin the siege, as soon as the Commander-in-Chief should see fit to move forward. Meanwhile, spies were employed to bring exact account of the enemy's lines of defensive works, on which they had been busily employed for the last three months, and very accurate we subsequently found their descriptions to be.

A day or two after my arrival, I rode to Alumbagh with Major T——, to examine that celebrated post. We went up to the top of the house, and had a good view of the ground in front, and of the enemy's network of trenches and batteries in that direction.

The country around was flat, but diversified with topes of fine mango trees; and, in the distance, we could discern the domes and turrets of some of the higher buildings in Lucknow. But our position before Lucknow was by no means so picturesque as the old one before Delhi. We were there so much closer to the city, and a ten minutes' canter from our mess to the top of the ridge gave us a full view of the whole place, and of all that was going on in the debateable land between us and the enemy. Here we were too far off to see anything of Lucknow, or of its lines of defence.

While we were looking at everything with our glasses, a round shot struck the parapet close to us, sent from the Yellow House, where Pandy had a battery, about 1,200 yards off; other round shot came flying about the house, or through the garden, and presently a sharp interchange of firing to the front showed that our advanced pickets were being attacked. Directly afterwards we heard the distant Pandy bugles, and a swarm of men, issuing from the advanced trenches, approached in front in skirmishing order, and towards our left in a dense mass, numbering several thousands. It was evident we were to be attacked in grand style. . The bugles still sounded the advance, and we could see a man on a grey horse, riding to the front, and followed by all of the most daring of the enemy, while loud shouts of "Chulo bhai!" ("Come on, brother!") were raised to encourage the mass of men who were advancing to attack a village on our left front, which was held by us in force. Soon we heard our camp bugles sounding; the 90th were under arms, and then Olphert's Battery and the Military Train Cavalry went off to the left, ready to take the advancing enemy in flank when an opportunity offered. The swarm of men came on very valiantly, till they were within range of our guns at the picket, and then these opened steadily upon them with round and grape, and Pandy was evidently much disinclined to come any farther, so he made off to his right, getting out of the fire of our guns, and began turning our left flank. Olphert's guns went to the front at a gallop, and, unlimbering within 400 yards, gave them such a dose, that they went to the right about at once, and numbers of dead bodies were afterwards found in the fields. Major T—— and I had ridden back to our own camp, thinking we might be wanted there; and we found, in effect, on arrival, that a swarm of skirmishers had thrown themselves into the cover near Jellalabad, and were firing at our men, who were returning the fire from the walls at a brisk rate. This went on for about two hours, and then Pandy found he had had enough of it, and drew off his men, having suffered rather severely for his morning's amusement, our casualties scarcely amounting to a dozen altogether.

About ten days after this a similar and final attack was made on the position, though this time it was more serious, and the chief effort was made on the right instead of the left. Swarms of rebels got round our right flank, and, keeping up a heavy fire on Jellalabad, even menaced the rear of our camp. They had the hardihood to approach the fort, carrying scaling ladders; but their courage failed them when they got within 200 yards, and they contented themselves with sending plenty of bullets at us from the cover all round. The General sent us up a reinforcement of cavalry and Horse Artillery, and as the enemy was well forward, our men got a chance at him; he was well pounded with grape, and the Military Train and Hodson's Horse, making a gallant charge, captured four guns, and cut up a large number of them. The attack lasted, in a desultory manner, nearly the whole of the day; and, having got much the worst of it, Pandy retired, as usual. We had some thirty casualties, I think, altogether. At length came the glad news that we were ready to advance, and on the 2nd of March, through a pelting rain, the Commander-in-Chief, with a considerable portion of the force brought up from the rear, passed along the road in front of our camp, and went off to the right, in the direction of the Dilkoosha.

We heard the sound of firing presently in that quarter, and soon the glad tidings came that the Dilkoosha park and palace had been seized by the Chief, after a sharp skirmish. We were to move there on the morrow, and then the siege would really begin at once. On the morning of the 3rd, the Artillery and Engineers parks, escorted by two regiments, marched with the whole of our brigade to join the Chief's camp. We had only four miles to go, but had to halt so many times for the immense train of stores forming the two parks, that we did not get into camp till eleven o'clock, having breakfasted under a tree on the road. We pitched in a grove of trees at Bibiapore, on the bank of the river, and about a mile in rear of the Dilkoosha, our camp being close to that of the head-quarters staff. While the tents were pitching, we got to the top of the large native house or palace at Bibiapore, and were now near enough to have a much better view of the work that lay before us than we could get at Alumbagh.

The picturesque-looking Martinière, quite close to us, was the enemy's most advanced position, and beyond it we could see part of the formidable lines of earthworks that he had constructed to oppose us.

The country around was flat, well cultivated, and beautifully diversified with numerous clumps of trees; the Goomtee River, more like our English than an Indian stream, went twisting and winding through the landscape, till it was lost in the distance, and a vague, indefinite area, apparently of endless extent, of mosques, temples, gardens, and buildings, told us that we were at last gazing on Lucknow.

On the 4th, General Franks' column, which had been fighting its way up through Oude from Benares, joined the grand army, and took up a position on the left of the Chief's force, stretching towards Alumbagh.

The same evening saw the commencement of the Engineering operations for the siege of Lucknow.

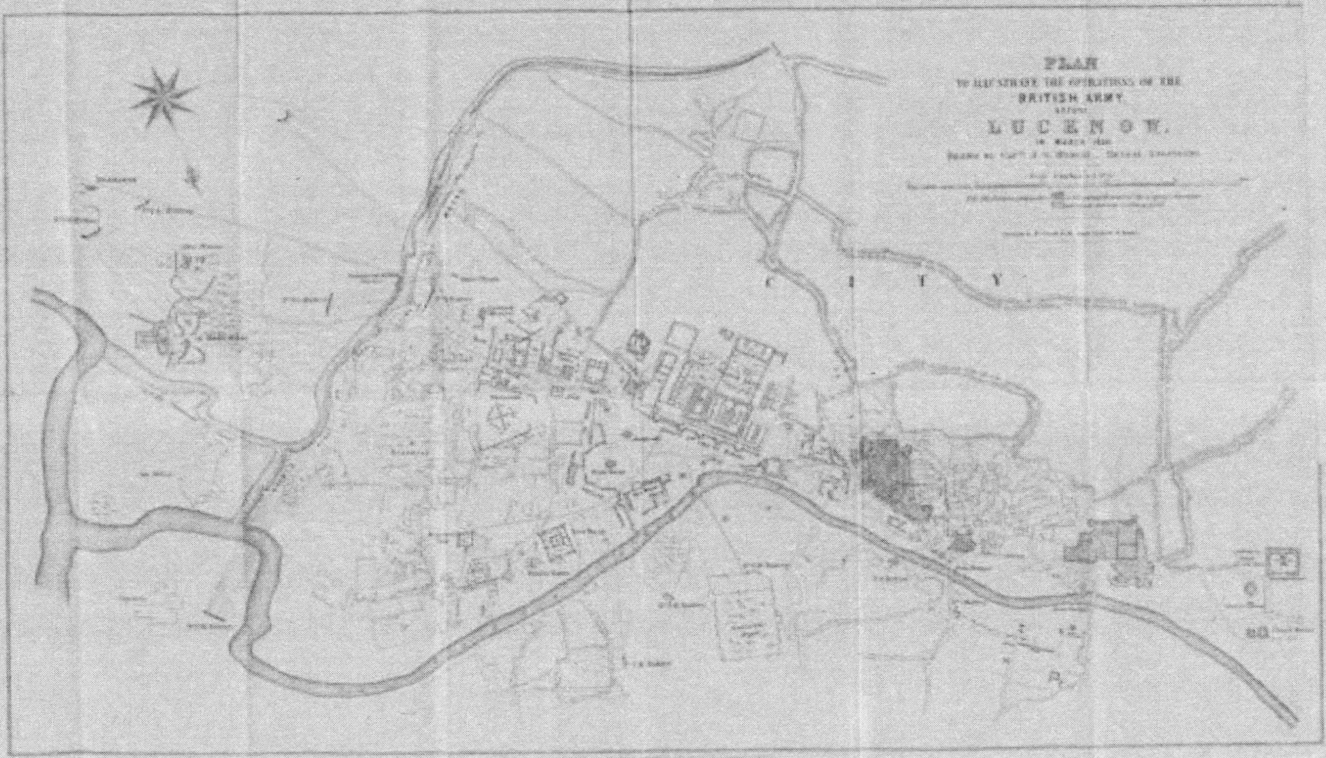
PLAN
BRITISH ARMY
LUCKNOW.
CITY

CHAPTER XIV.

THE SIEGE OF LUCKNOW.

LUCKNOW, the capital of the province of Oude, is one of the largest and most populous cities in the whole of India. It is situated on the Goomtee, a small stream, varying in width at this point from 40 to 100 yards, which rises in the lower hills of the Terai, and falls into the Ganges below Benares.

The whole area of the city is about twelve miles, and the population was ordinarily computed at 600,000 souls. The upper portion of the town is built on a long reach of the river flowing from N.W. to S.E., and the stream is here spanned in two places by a stone and iron bridge respectively. Three-quarters of a mile below the latter, the river makes a sudden bend, running towards the N.E., and then flowing round, joins a canal, which bounds the city to the S.W. and South. The Cawnpore Road crosses this canal by a masonry bridge at the Charbagh, and runs through the heart of the city for a length of two miles, up to the old Residency buildings, which stand on a high plateau of ground close to the river, and a little below the iron bridge.

The other great street of the town, the Huzrut Gunge, runs almost at right angles to the Cawnpore Road, and close to the bank of the river, from the bend above mentioned, upwards. Below the bend, this street or road still runs straight on, and then diverges into two branches, which cross the canal at different points, and lead to the Dilkoosha Palace and Martinière College. Between this main road and the curve of the river below the bend lie a mass of suburbs and isolated strong buildings, memorable as the scenes of numerous fights, as it was by this route that Havelock and the Commander-in-Chief relieved the Residency Garrison—working their way up the river rather than through the heart of the town, by the straight Cawnpore Road.

Along the line of the Huzrut Gunge lies a mass of large buildings, inhabited formerly by the Court and its officials, which, from their commanding situation and great height and extent, were capable of being made into strong defensive positions.

The Kaiser Bagh, with its squares of palaces and gardens, the residence of the King himself, lies on one side of the Huzrut Gunge; the Chutter Munzil, or Old Palace, lying on the other side, at the bend of the river. Proceeding still along this road up the river bank, we next come to the Residency buildings; then to the Muchee Bawun, an old and strong native fort; then to the great Emambara and adjoining mosque, through the Hosseinabad Palace; and passing through the suburbs at the N.W. end, emerge at the Moosa Bagh, a large garden and country house, just beyond the outskirts of the town.

The great mass of the city, therefore, lies between the Huzrut Gunge and the canal; but it was in the strong suburbs, and along the above line of palaces and high buildings that the advance of the British army took place, as a preferable course to involving ourselves in a series of endless street fights.

When the above strong positions were in our possession, the rest of the city, which was commanded by them, must fall as a matter of course.

The above description applies solely to the right or south bank of the river. On the other bank, however, there was an extensive suburb, almost in itself a town, but containing few buildings of importance. The road from the iron bridge ran through this suburb on to the old British cantonments at Muniao, four miles from the city, and branching from this road was the great road to Fyzabad, on the Gogra, seventy miles distant, and the second city in Oude.

Lucknow is not surrounded by a fortified wall, as is Delhi; but the rebels had well supplied its place, by the incessant labours of many thousands of workmen during the past three months. Knowing we should advance in the same general direction by which the last two advances had been made, they had strongly fortified every commanding building on the line of the Huzrut Gunge and in the suburbs near the river, and constructed three great lines of earthworks to bar our approach to the Kaiser Bagh, which might be considered as their citadel. The first of these lines ran along the canal, from the Charbagh Bridge to its junction with the river; the lower end being laboriously strengthened by a deep and straight cut made to the river from a point where the canal bed was shallow and tortuous. The canal served as a wet ditch: all the bridges across it were broken down, and a formidable rampart of earth, with strong bastions at intervals, was built on the farther bank.

The second line of works extended from the river, and passing in front of the Motee Mahal and the Mess House, rested on the Huzrut Gunge, joining it at the small Emambara. The third line of works immediately defended the Kaiser Bagh.

About 120 guns and mortars, of various calibres, were mounted on these works. But, besides these principal lines, the main roads and streets were blocked up at various points, and isolated batteries constructed to sweep down them. Almost every house was loopholed and fortified, and the immense labour that must have been bestowed in completing such a vast series of defences excited the surprise of every one who subsequently witnessed them. Faulty in general design they certainly were, and the fault was promptly taken advantage of in attacking; but had there been able leaders and courageous men behind those works, prepared to fight bravely for their cause, instead of an armed mob of rebels, distrusting each other, divided amongst themselves, and disheartened by repeated failures, the streets of Lucknow must have been dyed deeply with British blood, before our army could have gained entire possession of the city.

The chief defect of the lines of earthworks was that, resting, as they did, on a river which could easily be crossed, we should be able, from the other side of the river, to enfilade them, and take them all in reverse with our batteries.

In the two previous advances on Lucknow our armies had not been strong enough to carry out operations on both banks of the Goomtee simultaneously; and whether the enemy now thought that, as before, we did not intend to cross the river, or whether they had really made up their minds that we should not come to Lucknow a third time before the cold season, by which time they would have extended and perfected their works, is, of course, uncertain. We had advanced straight to the front before, because we had no help for it; and they seemed to fancy we must necessarily do so again, and run our heads against their bastions.

But, with 20,000 men and 180 guns, there was no occasion to waste men's lives in this way. A force was to cross the Goomtee, and render the enemy's lines untenable by the enfilade fire of our batteries. At the same time, the enemy's other flank was to be turned by the main attack, which was to advance along the Huzrut Gunge, and by the tremendous fire of our artillery, and a steady progress from house to house by sapping, was to seize the whole of this main street and the commanding houses along it, and press on steadily to the Kaiser Bagh. Threatened in front, and attacked on both flanks, the enemy would have no resource but to run, or to be cut to pieces.

Such was the plan of attack, and under the guidance of the Chief Engineer (Brigadier Napier), most ably was it carried out.

On the night of the 4th March, two bridges of casks were commenced across the Goomtee, not far from the site of our camp. By the morning one was completed; and a strong picket being thrown over, a small earthwork was constructed on the opposite bank to assist them in defending the bridge heads. No molestation was experienced during the night, but in the morning the enemy threw a few round shot at us from a village about 1,000 yards off, and a strong body of cavalry approached to see what we were at. They came pretty close, and had the picket kept itself well concealed in the hollow, they might have given them a volley at close quarters. As it was, the Sowars suddenly descried our men, and turning tail, went off as hard as they could gallop; the Minié bullets singing among them in very disagreeable proximity.

Some of our guns were brought down to the bank of the river, close to the bridge, and replied to the enemy's fire from the village when it began to be annoying. All that day we worked at the bridges, and the embankments that were to connect them with the shore on both sides.

On the night of the 5th I was sent down with a strong working party to complete both bridges, and have them ready for the passage of the column, that was to cross by two in the morning. We had only two shots sent at us during the night, which did no harm; and by twelve o'clock both bridges were ready, and I laid down to get some sleep before the column should arrive, which it did not do till four o'clock, some of the troops having missed their way in the dark.

General Outram, who was to command it, came down earlier, and having looked at the bridge, and expressed his approval, sat down on the ground, and began to smoke. It was still dark, when a troop of the 2nd Punjab Cavalry, which formed the advanced guard, began to cross, and very soon an incessant stream of guns, waggons, cavalry, infantry, carts, camels, and doolies choked up both bridges. The Commander-in-Chief himself came down to see the passage, which all occurred without accident. The troops formed up on the other side as fast as they crossed, but as day dawned the enemy saw them, and commenced firing from the village rather heavily. By six o'clock, however, the column was in motion. The heavy baggage was to follow after, when the enemy should be driven back, and the first halting ground chosen.

The events of the day consisted of a series of skirmishes, in which the rebels, who hardly attempted to stand, were driven from every village and tope they occupied, until, sweeping them before him up the river, Outram established himself firmly on the opposite side, and encamped on the old race-course.

The operations on the opposite side of the river being thus satisfactorily commenced, the Chief began to push on the main attack. For this purpose, the first operation was to obtain possession of the Martinière, and to drive the enemy over the canal.

During the 7th and 8th, therefore, batteries were

established to keep down the fire of the first line of bastions, and a formidable battery of 8-inch guns, belonging to the Naval Brigade, was erected near the Dilkoosha, which poured a storm of shot on the Martinière, and silenced the enemy's guns at that place. A sharp musketry contest, however, still continued between the 4th Punjab Rifles, who lined some old walls in front of the Dilkoosha, and the enemy's advanced pickets in a ruined village about 200 yards further on.

On the 9th, the Martinière was stormed and taken by the Highlanders and 4th Punjab Rifles, with trifling loss on our side. The enemy had withdrawn their guns, and fled precipitately across the nullah. On this day also, Captain Peel, commanding the Naval Brigade, was unfortunately wounded in the Dilkoosha Battery, and the army was deprived of his valuable services during the rest of the siege.

Meanwhile Outram had not been idle during the past three days. A powerful enfilade and reverse fire had been directed from his batteries across the river on the enemy's first line of entrenchments, under which the enemy found it impossible to live; and accordingly, on the 10th, the first line of works was entirely abandoned, to our great surprise;—a gallant young officer (Butler, of the 1st Fusileers) having swam across the nullah, and ascertained the fact.

The head-quarters camp, as well as the camp of the Engineer Brigade, was now advanced, and pitched close to the Martinière, where they remained till the end of the operations, the head-quarters of the General in command of the left or main attack being fixed at Bankes's House, immediately over the canal, and on the road (the Huzrut Gunge) along which the advance was to be pushed.

Since the 6th, I had been on the sick list, and was unable to take part in any of the preceding operations. On the 11th, however, having recovered, I was ordered down as Directing Engineer for the right portion of the main attack, and was told to go to the Secundra Bagh, which had been taken possession of that morning.

Major T—— and I first, however, went to find the Chief Engineer, to get my instructions, and, making our way to Bankes's House, we left our horses there, and proceeded on our search. We found our heavy batteries playing away on the enemy's defences in front, wherever they crossed the main road, the enemy making very little reply with his artillery, but keeping up a sharp musketry fire from the adjoining houses, especially the *Begum's Kothee*, which was the first of the series of strong houses on the left of the road that would have to be carried in succession to turn the right of the enemy.

Our old Delhi General, Sir A. Wilson, who now

commanded the artillery of the grand army, was moving about from one battery to another, observing the effect of the fire of our guns.

With some trouble we at last found our own Brigadier, and, having got my instructions, I rode off, and found my way to the Secundra Bagh, where a working party of Sappers, under two of our officers, had already proceeded.

This place, rendered memorable by the terrible fight that occurred here on the Chief's first advance to Lucknow, was, as its name denotes, a native garden, with an enclosure wall and various buildings, and summer houses inside. The breach by which the Chief had entered nearly three months before was still unrepaired, and the Sepoys evidently never contemplated a second time defending this place of ill omen.

L——, of the Engineers, my old companion at Delhi, and who was with me to-day, had witnessed the fight in November, having come down with Greathed's Column, and took me to see the courtyard in which 1,800 Sepoys were killed, having shut themselves up with no outlet of escape. L—— described the scene as a fearful one. Volley after volley from the Enfields was poured in through the doors and windows by our men, until at length a writhing mass of half dead men and corpses, piled five and six deep, showed that the massacre at Cawnpore was at last partially avenged. We found quantities of human hair and bones still lying about, and the smell, even now, was intolerable. So we both beat a rapid retreat, and climbing up on the roof of one of the other buildings, took a good survey of the enemy's works in front.

About 300 yards to our right front was a small, high, isolated building, the Kuddum Russool (Foot-step of the Prophet), and beyond this was the Shah Nujjeef, a large tomb or mosque, standing in a walled inclosure. Both posts were immediately outside the enemy's third line of works, which ran in front of the Motee Mahal (House of Pearls), the old Mess House of the 32nd Regiment, and the Tara Kothee, or Observatory. Seeing that the above two posts were very quiet, and that no firing was coming from them, L—— proposed that we should go and reconnoitre, and see if we could take possession of them. So with four of our native Sappers, L——, C——, and I went out of the Secundra Bagh; got well away to our right into some cover there was, and creeping up, revolvers in hand, found ourselves close to the Kuddum Russool. There appeared to be no one there, which was rather fortunate, as the little solitary door, and narrow winding steps, would have given a decided advantage in a personal contest to the person inside. So we quickly found ourselves in the little building, and looking down into the garden of the Shah Nujjeef; this also appeared to be abandoned. We did not, however, like to capture that with four men, as there might have been plenty of rebels inside the mosque itself; so we left our four Sappers to garrison our important conquest! and went back to the Secundra Bagh to ask for men to go and take the Shah Nujjeef; the Colonel commanding the post, however, demurred to do such a thing without orders, so I rode off to find out the General at Bankes's House, and having got his permission, returned with that to the Secundra Bagh. The Colonel, of course, no longer made any opposition, and ordered a detachment of 100 men, with 50 of our Sappers, to accompany us to the Shah Nujjeef. We met with no opposition; broke open two doors leading into the enclosure, and found the place evacuated; but, as we were only 200 yards from the enemy's second line of intrenchments, a sharp musketry fire was opened upon us from there, and we had an officer and one or two men wounded. We set the Sappers to work to make the place defensible; and, at my suggestion, 100 more men were thrown into the place.

As we were standing on the ramparts, pretty well protected from the enemy's musketry, we suddenly heard a great disturbance going on in the direction of our left attack. A very heavy fire of musketry went on, which increased rapidly in severity; shouts and cries were heard, and we saw thousands of rebels pouring out from the second line of works, apparently to defend some position in front; then we guessed, and rightly, that the *Begum's Kotee* was being stormed by our troops, and the first of the strong positions carried on the left attack. The firing lasted for some time, and then we saw the rebels in headlong flight, and apparently uncertain whether they were not to be pursued at once into their intrenchments.

About dark, L—— and C—— were relieved by Ch——, who came down and joined me with a working party of 50 Bengal Sappers, and he then told us that there had been a severe struggle on the left, and that Major T——, of the Engineers, was unfortunately amongst the wounded. The 93rd Highlanders and their native friends, the 4th Punjabees, had stormed the Begum's Kothee, after it had been breached by the heavy guns; the Sepoys, being taken by surprise, had not time to run, and nearly 500 of them were slaughtered. We also learnt that that fine cavalry officer, Major Hodson, had been severely wounded, while looking on as an amateur. He died the following day, and was a great loss to the service.

In the evening a strange accident occurred where we were. A badly aimed 8-inch shell, from one of our own batteries across the river, pitched right amongst the guard at one of our gateways; it ran down the sentry's musket, twisting the iron barrel into a most extraordinary shape, and sheared off the poor fellow's arm as completely as if it had been cut off with an axe. The man ran forwards nearly 200 yards, and then cried, "Oh, where's my arm?" I believe he afterwards died. Fortunately the shell did not burst, or the consequences would have been disastrous.

L—— and C—— went off to camp: I was not to be relieved till the morning, so Ch—— and I made ourselves comfortable for the night, he having brought dinner with him. About eight o'clock, however, the officer commanding the European detachment with us came up, and said he had orders to withdraw his men to the Secundra Bagh. I asked, "Why?" but he could not tell, and as I had no orders to retire, and thought perhaps the thing was a mistake, Ch—— and I determined to remain, and valiantly defend the place with the 50 Native Sappers, who were nearly all Poorbeahs, by the way, until we could get further instructions. So the Europeans marched off, and we posted our sentries as we thought best, and visited them every half hour.

Pandy was not likely to know that we were so weak, and it was not his custom to run his head against stone walls; still it was a large place to hold with so few men on a dark night, within 200 yards of the enemy, and I was not sorry when we were marched back safely, very early in the morning, having received an order to that effect in reply to my note.

It appeared afterwards that the Chief considered our position too far in advance of the main attack on the left, and as there was no necessity to risk anything, we were ordered to fall back.

G—— relieved me as Directing Engineer in the morning (the 12th), and I returned to camp.

Jung Bahadoor and his Goorkhas had arrived the previous day, and were ordered by the Chief to advance on our left, and hold the line of canal beyond Bankes's House. During this day and the 13th we were pressing our advance on the left, avoiding the main road, which was well defended by the enemy's bastions, and sapping through the houses instead; the heavy guns opening breaches where necessary, and the Sappers, supported by the infantry, pressing slowly but steadily on, and breaking open communications, so as to allow ample supports being furnished from the rear when required. The tremendous superiority of our artillery fire, supported as it was by Outram's enfilade, and cross fire from the other side of the river, effectually prevented any serious annoyance from the enemy's guns, but a hot fire of musketry was kept up, as we advanced, from the neighbouring houses, to which our covering parties in front were not slow to reply.

At length, by the evening of the 13th, we had sapped through, and taken possession of all the great buildings on the left as far as the *Emambara*, and the capture of that was fixed for the following morning.

Meanwhile, across the river, Outram having driven the enemy from his first line of works in our front by his fearful enfilade fire, had gradually cleared the rebels out of the suburbs, and, by the 11th, was in possession of the iron bridge. Powerful batteries were again established, and an awful fire, especially from mortars, kept up day and night on every position held by the enemy as far as the Kaiser Bagh itself.

In these extensive operations I do not pretend to give an exact account of every day's work, being, of course, only able to describe minutely what I saw myself; but the admirable letters of the *Times* correspondent have already put the public in possession of the events attending the siege of Lucknow, so that I shall easily be excused for not giving an exact journal of the siege.

CHAPTER XV.

THE SIEGE (CONCLUDED).

On the morning of the 14th of March I was ordered down, with a strong working party, and in company with several other Engineers, to join the assault on the Emambarra.

We marched down at daylight, carrying scaling ladders, powder bags, crowbars, &c., and passing through the courtyard of the Begum's Kothee and the other large buildings that had been taken beyond, found ourselves at length behind a wall with only the breadth of the road between us and the wall of the *Emambarra* enclosure. A battery of heavy guns was making a breach in the place at the distance of about thirty yards; the 8-inch shot, at this short distance, walking through three or four thick masonry walls in succession, as if they had been so much paper. The enemy were lining the top of the wall, and all the neighbouring houses, and keeping up a pretty hot fire, trusting, as usual, that some of their bullets would do mischief. The breach would not be practicable for some time, so after seeing that my party was all ready to advance, being drawn up in rear of the storming party of Brazyer's Seikhs, I sat down, and had a cheroot; at length, about nine o'clock, we got the order to advance, and in another minute were across the road, and scrambling through the breached walls, the rebels scuttling as usual a great deal too fast to be caught.

The enclosure was all ours; and I went into the building itself, which was full of chandeliers, mirrors, and an extraordinary assortment of ornaments, most of which were smashed by our men out of sheer mischief. The Seikhs and 10th Foot poured in through the great gateway into the road, and then we found that we had turned the 2nd line of entrenchments, and saw the rebels rushing away in every direction towards the Kaiser Bagh. Then began a series of skirmishes, accompanied by a perpetual pop-popping of musketry, as Pandy was driven out of one building after another, our men rushing down the road, or making their way from house to house on both sides. Meanwhile the Sappers were busy at work in loopholeing the parapets of the various buildings, to enable our men to reply to the fire from the houses, and in breaking open doors, &c., to enable our troops to push on, and to keep up communications with the rear. This sort of work lasted hour after hour, the troops in front still pushing on, and apparently resolved never to stop. Fighting,—there was none, in the ordinary sense of the term, as directly we got near him, Pandy bolted, but he kept up such an abominable fire from house tops, doors, and loopholes, that man after man went off wounded to the rear, while still we pushed on, our numbers getting thinner and thinner every minute, from the necessity of leaving men to keep possession of the places as fast as we took them. At length we found ourselves in the Cheenee Bazar, close to the Kaiser Bagh, and behind the enemy's 3rd line of works, and I really do not think there were 50 men with us. With some difficulty a halt was called, when the enemy seeing our small numbers, or not having been able to run away quickly enough, came round on both flanks, and let drive at us at 20 yards distance. We drew swords, pulled out our revolvers, and rushed at them, on which they fled; and just then, up came a lot of our Goorkhas, and charging along the 3rd line of intrenchments, cleared the enemy out very speedily, though not without losing several men. General Franks now came up, followed by strong supports; and the Chief Engineer, having also joined, a consultation was held in a gateway, as to what was to be done. When the advance took place in the morning, the only intention was to storm the Emambara, but our men had pushed on so fast, and Pandy had run at such a surprising rate, that we were now at the Kaiser Bagh, and perfectly ready to go in and take it. So more troops were sent for from the rear, and G——, of the Engineers, was ordered to bring up men from the Secundra Bagh and the positions on the right, and take possession of the buildings towards the river, so that the whole line of attack might advance simultaneously. I was ordered to stay where we were till I had fortified the gateway, which was the farthest point of our advance along the main road. While we were talking together, the report of a musket sounded quite close to us, and poor Captain Wall, of the 87th, who was sitting next to me, fell forward on his face with a loud cry. He had been shot through the spine by a Sepoy, concealed in a house on the opposite side of the road, and died about an hour afterwards. It was so close, that a splinter grazed the back of my hand. Shortly afterwards an explosion of loose powder took place in the road below, and scorched an officer and some men severely. Several explosions occurred in the course of the day, and killed or wounded many men.

As soon as more men had come up from the rear, the advance was made to the Kaiser Bagh, through the large court of the great mosque on our left. The whole place was, before long, in our possession, and an immense amount of plunder obtained by the troops. Having done the work I was ordered to do, I went into the Kaiser Bagh, and witnessed the extraordinary scenes going on. A fierce rattle of musketry was still being carried on between the rebels, from the surrounding houses, and men from the tops of the buildings in the palace squares. The Kaiser Bagh itself consisted of a series of courts and gardens laid out with rectangular walks, trees, shrubs, statues, &c., and surrounded by buildings of a light, elegant appearance outwardly, and the general effect of the whole, interspersed as it was with marble summer houses, tanks, and fountains, was indescribably picturesque. There seemed a quaint mixture of Italian and Oriental architecture, which made by far the prettiest sight that I had yet seen in an Indian city, and which would not have been unworthy of the residence of a European monarch.

Now, however, house after house was being plundered of its furniture and miscellaneous contents, and swords, in rich scabbards, embroidered cloths, shawls, ornaments, and a most extraordinary and varied assortment of European articles of every kind and description, guns, clocks, books, &c., were spread about in every direction. No order had been issued against plundering, and there was no doubt that an immense booty, in hard cash and

and jewels alone, was obtained that day. Part of the buildings were on fire, probably ignited by the enemy in their flight. I cut off the communication with the main range, by cutting through the roof at the top, and blowing down some of the supporting pillars; but the fire at the other end went on smouldering or burning for two or three days afterwards, before it was entirely extinguished.

After a long and fatiguing day's work, I returned to camp about 8 p.m., and slept like a top, after the exciting adventures of the day.

On the 15th no advance was made on the left, but during this and the three following days Outram crossed the iron bridge, and, thus effecting a junction with the main force, advanced; and, after a series of skirmishes, the Residency, Muchee Bawan, and their strong portions, were taken. At the same time an advance was made up the Cawnpore road on the 17th, and a communication through the heart of the city effectually established with our old position at the Alumbagh.

The rebels were now flying in thousands from the N. and N.W. ends of the city, and by the 18th every strong post was in our hands, except the Moosa Bagh, where a large body of men had collected, with several guns, prepared to make a final stand.

On the previous day a disastrous explosion occurred

in removing some thirty cart-loads of powder from the Jumunia Bagh; and Captain Clark, of the Royal Engineers, Lieut. Brownlow, of our corps, one of the most promising young officers we had, with nearly thirty European and Native soldiers, lost their lives. I was employed, that night, in getting up some heavy mortars to the Residency, to shell the rest of the city, and in the morning had my first view of that famous position. The houses, walls, &c., were, however, so battered about by shot, and so injured by the rebels after the evacuation, that it was difficult to understand the site merely from the descriptions I had read; but, some days afterwards, I had an opportunity of going over the whole ground with Captain H——, of the Engineers, who had been a very active participator in the defence, and he explained the locality to me. That such a position should have been held for so long, in the face of so many difficulties, filled me with admiration. But I need not dwell farther upon this, as so many narratives of the celebrated siege have already been given to the public. The admirably commanding position of the ground, and the want of shells on the part of the rebels, must have been great aids to the gallant garrison; but nothing can detract from the merit of the defence of a few houses, by a handful of men against 60,000 enemies.

On the morning of the 19th, I was ordered, with a strong working party of Sappers, to join the column, with which Sir J. Outram was to attack the Moosa Bagh.

We were at first ordered to remain with the heavy guns in the rear, but were soon ordered to the front, to open a road for the light guns through a thick wall that stopped our advance. It took us some time to break through this, and then the column pushed on, as we heard the rebels had already begun to retreat. I rode on ahead, and joined the General's Staff, and we soon found ourselves at the Moosa Bagh, a large Native garden, with a fine house or palace at one end of the enclosure. The Horse Artillery went to the front, and the rebels went fast to the rear, not attempting to hold the house or garden, and abandoning all their guns.

The Cavalry went on in pursuit, and the Infantry followed in skirmishing order, through the fields and groves of trees. We followed, in this manner, for some six miles further, cutting up 200 or 300 stragglers and fugitives, and capturing fourteen guns.

Another column was to have co-operated with ours from the Alumbagh direction, but we saw nothing of it, and I believe it missed its way.

Our force returned to the city after a long day's work, and this was the last day's fighting I saw at Lucknow.

The city might now be considered our own, but it was quite unsafe to wander through the streets at any distance from the pickets, and two young officers were murdered in this way.

On the 21st information was received that a gang of desperadoes had returned to the city, and with two guns had actually taken up a position in the very heart of the place. A party of the 42nd Highlanders and 4th Punjabees was ordered to dislodge them, which was not effected without a very severe struggle, several of our men being killed, and the Commandant and second in command of the 4th Punjab Rifles being desperately wounded.

This was the last skirmish that took place, and with this ended the siege of Lucknow, which may be said to have commenced from the passage of General Outram's force across the Goomtee on the 6th.

It was, therefore, of about the same duration as the siege of Delhi, exactly six months previously. Here, however, all resemblance ceased.

The splendid army before Lucknow in March, 1858, contrasted strangely with the small force assembled at Delhi in September, 1857, scraped together with the greatest difficulty, composed of so many miscellaneous elements, and worn out by three months of incessant fighting, at the most trying season of the year. And a greater difference still existed in the tremendous Artillery wielded by the rebels at Delhi, with the immense supplies of ammunition they drew from our own magazines, and the feeble resistance offered at Lucknow by their wretched Native guns to the most powerful collection of siege artillery employed by our army, which India had ever seen brought together in the field.

The struggle, therefore, at Lucknow was far less arduous than that at Delhi. Nevertheless, the extent of the operations made it hard work for the troops, and we had not a man too many. The defect in the enemy's lines of defence has already been pointed out, and the able manner in which this was taken advantage of—the efforts of the besieged being paralyzed by the infernal fire from across the river, and the operations of the left attack so vigorously but judiciously pushed on—must ever be the subject of admiration on the part of the military student of this campaign. This great success was achieved, too, with an incredibly small loss, about 700 killed and wounded forming the total of our casualties. We captured 120 guns, an immense quantity of ammunition, a large amount of treasure, and stores of all sorts, and deprived the rebellion of its greatest prestige, by the complete re-occupation of a capital which had so long defied our power.

These results being achieved, the grand army now broke up. A powerful force, under Sir H. Grant, was left at Lucknow; a column, under Sir E. Lugard, marched southwards to Azimgurh; the remainder of the army, under General Walpole, accompanied by the Commander-in-Chief himself, marched northwards to effect the conquest of Rohilcund, in co-operation with the column, which had been collected in the north at Roorkee, and which now received orders to cross the river.

The Engineer Brigade was nominally broken up; but the Chief Engineer and a large number of officers (of whom I was one) still remained at Lucknow, to arrange for the proper occupation and defence of the city. The troops were quartered in the large buildings and palaces, and generally on the line parallel to the river from the Moosa Bagh, along the Huzrut Gunge to the canal. The General Hospital was established in the Chutter Munzil; the commissariat stores in the Motee Mahal; the ordnance stores in the lesser Emambarra. All these posts were made defensible as far as could be done at so short notice; and, at the same time, a regular scheme was prepared, by which the permanent occupation of the city was to be secured.

A large military fort, to include the Muchee Bawan and the great Emambarra, was to be made, so as to command the stone bridge on the one side, and to overawe the town on the other.

A smaller fort also designed for the iron bridge, and a third was to be built at the Residency. The houses all round these were to be swept away for a distance of 500 yards; and two great roads, 150 feet wide and perfectly straight, were to run from the principal fort, through the heart of the city, in different directions. The most urgent of these works were at once put in hand, and early in April I was appointed Garrison Engineer of Lucknow, to carry out the above design.

Writing, as I now am, in the month of July, the events that followed the close of the Lucknow campaign are already matter of history. Rohilcund has been conquered; the Central India field force has captured Calpee and Jhansee; and the Gwalior disaster, which at one time looked very serious, has, by the rapidity with which it has been repaired, given the natives a striking proof of our energy and strength.

How different was our position in the same month of last year! It was then that affairs wore their very blackest aspect. Our force before Delhi could barely hold its own. The garrison at Lucknow was closely besieged, and it seemed as if nothing but a miracle could rescue them. The fearful massacre at Cawnpore had occurred. All communication along the Grand Trunk Road between Delhi and Allahabad was cut off. Nearly the whole of the N.W. Provinces were in the hands of the rebels.

In looking back on the general events of the campaign, it is necessary to remember that the force of circumstances exercised a decided influence over the conduct of the war. Could we but have united the scattered fragments of our European force into one, or even two armies, we should have had a force in the field that would have been strong enough to crush anything that the rebels could ever have brought into the open. But such a course would have compelled us to weaken ourselves at nearly every point, and the insurrection must have become general. Purely military considerations, which would have pointed to a concentration of our scattered troops, were compelled to give way to the importance of maintaining our prestige; and often the bold and resolute bearing of a few British officers saved a whole district to the Government, or postponed an explosion until it was no longer dangerous. Delhi being wrested from our hands, with its great arsenal and the reputation of its name, our first efforts were naturally directed to the capture of that place. It was then thought that this would easily and promptly be effected, and that with the fall of Delhi the mutiny would receive a sudden check. When it was found that we had embarked in an undertaking, to which our available strength for a long time was wholly inadequate, it was then too late to abandon it.

The raising of the siege would have been the signal for universal revolt. But though this hampered the action of our only army, it yet concentrated the mutineers very much in one place, and gave us a single point to look to, instead of a hundred, to be undertaken at once, and in the most unfavourable time of the year for moving.

Our great danger was, that the rebels, leaving a sufficient number to guard Delhi, should have detached columns strong enough to cut off our communication with the Punjab.

Had our faithful ally, the Puttiala Raja, been defeated, or had Umballa and Kurnaul been attacked, the army at Delhi, barely sufficient to hold its own, with the help of all the supplies and reinforcements that could be spared from the Punjab, would have been isolated from its communications, and must have raised the siege, and cut its way back to Lahore.

Next to this, the greatest of our dangers was the chance of the tranquillity of the N.W. frontier being disturbed, Had Dost Mahommed died, had one of his bigoted and ambitious sons raised the green flag, and proclaimed a religious war, the Punjab might have been inundated by thousands of warlike tribes, and the times of Nadir Shah have again been revived. But the Chief Commander of the Punjab knew the importance of Peshawur. Its loss would have been greater than the loss of Delhi. So, though every other cantonment in the Punjab was weakened to supply General Wilson's army, the force at Peshawur was maintained intact; the few partial risings that occurred were at once put down; and while the political affairs of the frontier were managed with consummate address by the Commissioner, Colonel Edwardes, the military arrangements were as ably directed by that fine soldier, General Cotton.

Down country, in a similar way, the course of the campaign was not under our control.

The imminent peril of the Cawnpore garrison required that every available man should be sent up to their relief, and when that, alas! came too late, the similar danger of the Lucknow garrison compelled us to divert our attention from our main line of communication to the north, and cross the Ganges to succour Lucknow.

The first relief was only a partial one, and occurred almost simultaneously with the fall of Delhi. Our success at the latter place set free 3,000 men, to move down country to the assistance of the Commander-in-Chief; but it released, on the other hand, at least 30,000 rebels to strengthen the hands of their brethren at Lucknow. And the efforts of the besiegers, after Havelock and Outram had joined the Residency garrison, were more strenuous than before.

It was not till the end of November that the Commander-in-Chief, with a portion of the reinforcements from England, and aided by the Delhi column, could extricate the whole of the garrison, and turn his attention to the real objects of the campaign. The decisive victory at Cawnpore left him free to move up country, and by his junction, at Futtyghur, with the 2nd Delhi column, under Colonel Seaton, the Grand Trunk Road was once more open, and the plan of the campaign could be distinctly mapped out. With the Doab once more in our possession, and the Ganges and Jumna well watched by detachments, the conquests of Oude and Rohilcund by the Commander-in Chief in person, and of the revolted districts of Central India by the columns set in motion from Bombay, became purely military movements, and were all happily accomplished. Every strong place, every town to whose name a prestige could be attached, has been torn from the rebels' hands; and though the Guerilla war, that yet remains to us, may be troublesome and harassing, the power that exterminated the Pindarrees will not fail in this task.

CHAPTER XVI.

THE CAUSES OF THE MUTINIES.

So much has already been written about the origin of the mutinies, that though a great diversity of opinion may exist on various points of the question, most of those who are competent to give an opinion on the subject, and are not led away by prejudice or party feeling, have pretty well made up their minds on the main features of the case.

If I venture to make a few remarks on the subject, it is more with a view of collating other men's ideas than of obtruding my own. An experience of ten years, in which I have seen both regular and irregular troops on service and in quarters, without ever belonging to either, may at least serve to render me, to some extent, a competent and unprejudiced witness in the case.

Some still insist that it has been a military mutiny, and a military mutiny only; others will have it that it has been a popular insurrection. The truth seems, as usual, to lie between the two extremes. It was undoubtedly, at first, a mutiny of the Bengal Regular

Native Army. But in all countries, and in the East especially, there is a large class of men whose instincts are adventurous, and who are ready to take advantage of any great convulsion of society to serve their own ends. These were gradually drawn into the vortex; and finally, as the revolt of the Poorbeah army became universal, it naturally drew into it the whole of that class from which the Poorbeah army was drawn. But that any such feeling was ever aroused, as could be dignified with the name of a national movement, is certainly untrue, with perhaps the single exception of the Province of Oude. The great bulk of the people were everywhere passive.

In every country where the vast majority of the population is agricultural, revolution is easy. Witness France and the whole of the East. In commercial countries the reverse is notorious: and the reason is evident. An agricultural community has less intelligence, and cares less for political questions, than the dwellers in cities. Provided they are not taxed beyond a certain limit, they are very willing to accept any change of rulers; their scattered situation renders them unable to effect that union of action required for a special object, and they usually accept quietly the dictation of the cities. But commerce multiplies intelligence, and multiplies cities. These, however fiercely political they may be, counteract one another by their mutual jealousy, and commercial men know well that revolutions paralyze commerce.

There is no novelty in these observations. I only adduce them to indicate and to account for the passive indifference of nine-tenths of the people in the late war. They knew that people must eat, whether black or white; they went on sowing their fields, certain that the corn would be sold, and that they should have to give up a share of it, in the shape of tax or contribution; and, unfortunately for us, they recognized their present prosperous and peaceful condition as the normal state of affairs, the present generation having forgotten the time when, under a weak Native government, hordes of Pindarrees looted and burnt their villages, murdered the men, and carried off the women and children into slavery.

Nothing is more remarkable than the entire absence of pretext of any real grievance, in the different manifestoes put forward by the rebel leaders. With that candour and ingenuousness which always leads Englishmen to exaggerate their own faults and "wash their dirty linen in public," we all knew and proclaimed that there were serious defects in our government of India, though labouring earnestly after their removal. That torture did exist to a certain extent; that the structure of our law was too complex; that our police system was, in many districts, a failure;

that not much had been done for education; that more might have been done for public works; that subalterns, fresh from school, often called natives "niggers," and addressed the *argumentum ad hominem* rather oftener than was, perhaps, needful: these things were never denied. But were they felt as hardships by the natives? Did they not know that the little finger of their own rulers was thicker than the thigh of the white man?—and that white whips were, at any rate, preferable to black scorpions? Certainly no such grounds for disaffection were ever put forth; and the most laughable and childish pretexts of their caste being broken, and their being forcibly made Christians, were the sum and substance of every proclamation. That some other cause than the greased cartridges lay at the bottom of this violent explosion is undoubtedly true; and it will be the aim of Government to find out who were the stirrers-up of the Sepoy mind. Perhaps some of the chukladars of Oude, or the hangers-on of the court of Lucknow, who suddenly found their power destroyed by the annexation; perhaps the influence of Persia, or of the unseen agent that pulls the wires of that monarchy, may yet be traced in it. All this has yet to be discovered.

But the alleged reason for the revolt, amongst the Sepoys themselves, was the greased cartridge, and that alone.

The establishment of the Rifle Depôts at Umballa, Sealkote, and elsewhere, favoured the spread of this feeling and the plans of the seditious, in an extraordinary manner, by bringing a few men from so many regiments together at the same place. So that at one of the depôts thirty-four regiments were represented, and the men who had been thus collected for instruction in the new rifle became active emissaries of sedition on their return to their regiments.

But whatever means were used by the active originators of the mutiny to excite the feelings of the Sepoys, it is impossible to deny that had there not been a general unhealthy state of mind throughout the Native army itself, the pernicious poison of sedition would not have been so rapidly imbibed; and the absurd fears that Government intended to interfere with their caste, or convert them, by force, to Christianity, would have quickly died away, or, at the utmost, produced one or two partial and local outbreaks. But, in truth, the greased cartridges was merely the match that exploded the mine which had, owing to a variety of causes, been for a long time preparing. Some of these I will briefly touch upon, merely to sum up opinions which are now pretty generally acceded to by all who know anything of the subject. It is difficult to estimate the exact order of their importance, and I therefore merely put them down as they occur to me.

1. The over-centralizing policy of our Government, by which all power was taken out of the hands of commanding officers. This, in an Asiatic community, whether civil or military, is undoubtedly a mistake. It arose, of course, from the anxious desire of Government to protect its Native soldiers against the possible caprices of commanding officers; the consequence has been, that the Sepoy looked to "Government," or the "Regulations," for his future prospects of advancement, and not, as he ought to have done, to his immediate superiors. Those strong feelings of personal attachment from the soldier to his officer, the result partly of love and partly of fear, which formerly were common, and which are the very life-blood of a regiment, at last became quite rare, and almost unknown in the regular army.

2. Akin to this was the seniority system of promotion in the Native ranks, which gave no stimulus to exertion, and made Native officers of old and decrepid men, only fit to be invalided.

3. The withdrawal of so many European officers from their regiments for Staff duties, which rendered those officers who were left dissatisfied with their position, and only anxious to get away from the regiment as soon as possible.

The above three causes combined substituted, in fact, a *system* for *men*. The army became a well-constructed machine, capable of being put in motion by any one who could set certain levers to work, and without any of the *esprit de corps* enthusiasm for the profession and personal atttachment to their officers, which, in an army of mercenaries, go far to supply the place of patriotism.

The lever *was* worked by clever scoundrels, and that lever was *fanaticism*, and the whole machine has gone to pieces in consequence. It is impossible to argue from cause to effect when fanatics are the subject of your argument, or to suppose that because certain causes produce certain effects with sane people that they will do so in this case. So that ever since the mutiny broke out, it has been accompanied by such a curious series of events, that has fairly puzzled every one who did not consider that fanaticism is, in fact, insanity.

Regiments that had no chance of escape mutinied, and were cut to pieces; others that might have mutinied at any time without let or hindrance, remained faithful till success was no longer possible, and then broke out, and met with a like fate.

In many instances, as is well known, Sepoys shot their officers on parade, or murdered them in their own houses; in others, they protected them and their families, supplied them with money, and parted from them with tears. Nor did this difference of treatment apparently in the least depend on the difference of character in the officers themselves.

When the mutiny first occurred, it was attributed by many at home to want of kindness and harsh treatment on the part of the European officers towards their Sepoys. But this calumny was soon silenced when it was seen in how very many cases it was evidently false. Major Spencer, for instance, of the 26th Native Infantry, had been twenty-five years in his regiment, and was universally known as a kind and good officer. He was murdered in the lines of his own regiment under circumstances of the deepest treachery. Colonel Fisher, of the 15th Irregular Cavalry, had spent the whole of his life in India, was on the most intimate and kindly terms with every man in his regiment, and treated his Native officers almost as brothers. Yet though his men did not actually kill him themselves, they gave him no warning, and stood by quietly, while the men of another regiment cut him down. Many other instances might be adduced, which show, I think, not that the natives are incapable of gratitude and attachment, but simply that the madness produced by fanaticism is so strong as to outweigh every other feeling. We have had instances enough of this in Ireland to prevent our looking upon it as anything peculiar to the natives of India. And while I am no apologist for the cold-blooded atrocities that disgraced the mutineers, I would bid those who would vote for indiscriminate bloodshed, and engender a warfare of race against race, to look back in history, and read the crimes of the French Revolution and the Irish Rebellion.

4. The next cause that is now universally admitted to have contributed to the mutiny was the enlistment of so large an army from almost entirely one class of men. The Poorbeahs of Oude and Hindostan in general constituted three-fourths of the Bengal Regular Army. And though divided into Hindoos and Mussulmans, and subdivided into two or three castes or classes, there was yet a strong feeling of union amongst them all, until at length the army became quite a close service, open only to the few favoured classes. The strength of this feeling was not known, until the attempt of the Government to introduce 200 Seikhs into each regiment of the line, after the annexation of the Punjab, failed so signally.

Though many commissioned officers certainly did object to having men of lower caste, smaller stature, and less cleanly appearance than the regular Poorbeah, yet others saw the wisdom of the measure, and did their best to insure its success; but in vain. The unfortunate Seikhs who were introduced were so bullied, and led such a life of annoyance amongst the combined Poorbeahs, that they were glad to beat a retreat.

5. That the proportion of Native to European soldiers has been allowed to exceed by very much the safe maximum, is also evident. The European soldier, however, is a very expensive article in this country, and we cannot hold India by main force of Europeans alone, or the revenues of the country would be absorbed by the expenses of the army. But, whatever happens, we must undoubtedly have a much larger European army in India in future than we ever had before.

I believe I have now touched on the five principal causes of the mutiny, in the truth of which all are pretty well agreed; or, rather, on those causes which predisposed the Sepoy mind to revolt.

There are others, undoubtedly, but most of them are controversial, and would lead me into prolonged dissertations, which I have no mind to inflict on the reader. But after we have enumerated every possible cause, one yet remains, undeterminate in its nature, but probably more powerful than all the others put together:—I mean that antagonism of race, colour, and religion which has always existed between the black and white man, which makes a broad line of demarcation between the two, not to be effaced by any individual efforts, and which, when the two parties stand in the relation of conquerors and conquered, as they do in India, requires to be borne in mind, to be acted on as a fact that no philanthropical theories can surmount, and the period of whose future termination is known only to God.

CHAPTER XVII.

THE FUTURE ORGANIZATION OF THE ARMY.

In spite of the many intelligent men who advocate a contrary view, I fear that few who have served through any part of the last campaign, and who know what the present state of the country is, will have much hesitation in saying that we cannot do without a Native army in India.

I do not care to discuss, just now, whether they shall be called Police, or Regulars, or Irregulars; I simply mean, that to hold India as it is at present, as it has been for fifty years past, and is likely to be fifty years hence, we must have a large body of trained and disciplined natives, armed with fire-arms, and commanded by European officers.

It is quite possible that, at some unknown epoch, when a rigorous disarmament, carried on for a long series of years, has broken down the spirit of the people, or converted them all into an enlightened agricultural and commercial community, that peace may be kept by special constables, or policemen in blue coats, glazed hats, and polished staves. But, unfortunately, while the question has been theoretically discussed with great eagerness by newspaper editors, members of parliament, and a host of pamphleteers, the local governments have had to suppress the mutiny and quiet the country, and have practically settled the question, by raising, training, and arming some 50,000 Native soldiers.

Moreover, I do not hesitate to say, that it has been over and over again seen, in the late campaign, that for war in India, a mixed force of Europeans and natives is better than one of Europeans alone.

The British soldier is a splendid fellow under certain conditions. Feed him well, do not over-work or over-march him, and bring him into the *open* with any number of enemies against him, and he will thrash them, unless the odds are hopeless, and then he will try his best. But on a long and tedious campaign, in a foreign country, and under a trying climate, he is very helpless. His officers must see to everything, and do everything for him. He will make a long march at a stretch to reach a battle-field: but a series of long marches knocks him up; he cannot get on without good food and liquor, or without proper shelter; and is, in fact, not a good campaigning animal. Now this is just what the Indian soldier is: with a bag of flour, and a brass pot to draw water from the wells as he passes, he will be perfectly cheerful and comfortable, and will march at the rate of 30 miles a day. It is clear, therefore, that for many purposes he is invaluable, if only to save the lives of the Europeans; and do without him I maintain we cannot.

We have had a Sepoy army which, for 100 years, has done us excellent service; its former history contains numerous proofs of fidelity and bravery, even when both were most strongly tried. It has turned upon us at last, from a variety of causes, the remedy of which lies in our own hands. By the light of experience (a fearful one, certainly) we see wherein we have failed. The sword that has served us well for so long has cut our hand by our own careless handling. Shall we, then, throw it away as useless in future? I do not see the logic of an affirmative reply.

If the causes or incentives of the mutiny, which I have indicated in the last chapter, be admitted as correct, they will show us what we ought to avoid in attempting to reorganize our Native army.

1. Let ample power be given to commissioned officers of Native regiments. A Native understands a despotism, the power of an individual will, "Do this, and he doeth it;" he does *not* understand courts-martial, regulations, and a divided administration. Choose commanding officers carefully and well; then

give them great powers, and judge them by the results. Is the regiment in a thoroughly efficient state for service? Are the men well-disciplined, skilled in the use of their arms, promptly obedient, and well-disposed? If so, be not too careful to inquire into the bye-laws and *modus operandi* by which these important ends have been obtained. One man has one way of working; another has another, probably equally good. If you attempt to systematize too much, you cramp individual action, and gain no good result. The over-centralizing policy of our Government is now universally admitted. No one who reads, day after day, the long strings of orders issued by "the Right Honourable the Governor-General in Council," or "H. E. the Commander-in-Chief," can doubt that the time and attention of those important personages are unnecessarily taken up by petty details which could easily be settled, not merely by the local governments, but by their subordinate officials.

When the first result of the mutinies was to a great extent to isolate the local governments from the central authority at Calcutta, it was remarkable with how much greater rigour those governments acted; and how well every department got on, when emancipated, even for a time, from the deadly thraldom of continual check and control and the weight of an enormous official correspondence. It is not too much to say that the motto for government in the East should be in direct opposition to the cant cry at home, "Measures, not men." In India it ought to be, "Men, not measures."

If this is so in civil matters, how much more is it not the case in the army, where success depends so much on promptitude and vigour?

If the annual inspections of regiments by Brigadiers and Generals were severe and minute, it is impossible than an inefficent Commanding Officer could do much harm; he would be detected, and should be at once removed.

To insure this rigid inspection, it might be as well to have Inspecting Generals specially appointed for this work, and they should be selected from the ablest men in the service; not necessarily the best Generals in the field, but the men who are best provided with the faculty of organization and administrative detail—Soults rather than Neys.

There is no doubt the commands of regiments should be the ordinary prizes of the service, and should never be given to inefficient men. They are the executive officers—the working men,—on whom the efficiency of the army depends. Not one man in ten is fit for the command of a European regiment; but not one European in fifty is fit for the command of a Native regiment. Experience has amply proved that four or five good European officers are enough for a Native regiment, even when on service; and if all young officers were posted to European regiments when they first came out, and transferred from them, by selection, to the Native corps; if, in fact, the so-called irregular system was substituted for the regular, I have no doubt that we should have taken at least one step towards securing a really good and reliable Native army.

2. Let the best men be selected for Native officers, seniority being only *one* claim for a man's promotion. Many officers, seeing that the Native officers of the late army have given no help whatever to Government, would abolish the grades altogether; but this is certainly a mistake. The Native officers can be made, and ought to be made, the connecting link between the European officer and his men; and it is to them he should look for the efficiency and loyalty of the Sepoys. No one in his senses could suppose that the old Subahdars and Jemadars, who were most of them only fit for the pension list, would be any assistance to Government in a crisis. They were simply so many old men, rewarded for having served a certain number of years. In the Punjab Irregular force, on the contrary, it is rare to see a white-haired Native officer. They are selected from men in the

prime of life, fit for hard work; and they *really* command their companies, and are invaluable to the commanding officer. Every method should be tried of still more bringing them into close connection with the European officers, and, to a certain extent, detaching them from the men; and respectable Native gentlemen, of good families, might often, I think, get commissions, as outsiders, with advantage.

3. Regimental duty should not be made a punishment and a loss to the European officer. If so many officers are wanted with a regiment, let them have duties to perform, and pay them well. If they are not wanted, let them be taken away from the regiments altogether, and a Staff corps formed for Staff purposes. But if all officers were, as above suggested, attached to European regiments, and selected for the Native regiments, this difficulty would cease.

4. Enlist from all castes and classes; do not exclude the high caste Rajpoot, nor the low caste Sudra; in fact, do not let the word caste be mentioned.

Announce that the service is open to *all*, that the pay is so much, and that implicit obedience to every order will be insisted upon. The advantages of the Company's salt would go a long way to make men oblivious of their caste prejudices, if they found every attempt to set up those prejudices above the rules of the service and their duties as soldiers steadily resisted. Whether complete regiments should be formed of one caste or class; whether, if they are mixed in the same regiment, the companies should still be classified, or whether all should be mixed indiscriminately together; whether regiments should be raised as militia, and kept for local purposes in general; or whether, on the contrary, Punjabees should be employed in Hindustan, and Poorbeahs in the Punjab,—are questions on which opinion is much divided, and on which I would not venture to decide. But I think they are all subordinate to the one principle, that caste must everywhere and always be made subservient to military duty.

5. The exact proportion that the Native army should bear to the European also admits of wide difference of opinion. But all are agreed that the number of Europeans was unduly small, and must be largely increased. That European artillerymen only should be allowed is also, I think, a very advisable precaution; and I would take away guns from every Native Prince or Chief throughout the Empire, and prohibit the possession of artillery by any, under the severest penalties. No one who knows the importance attached by Natives to artillery, and the confidence that the possession of the veriest old honeycombed bit of iron that could by courtesy be termed a gun, gives to parties of armed rebels, who without

it would at once disperse, will, I am convinced, think this precaution needless.

It is unnecessary, too, to point out that all forts, arsenals, and magazines of every kind should be guarded exclusively by Europeans.

With these precautions, and a rigorous Arms Act, enforced by periodical searches and heavy penalties, there would be little risk of another insurrection.

I say nothing of kind treatment to the Natives, because any one that asserts, either in newspaper or on platform, that the Government has not steadily and unceasingly directed its efforts for many years past to the welfare of the Indian people, and that it has not been aided as a body by its officials, both civil and military, with a zeal and energy unknown and uncheered by public approbation at home, in a deadly climate, and removed from nearly all the social pleasures that made life agreeable, only slanders his countrymen, and betrays his own ignorance.

Errors there have been in plenty, but, as a whole, the government of the East India Company has been, without doubt, one of the purest and most enlightened in the world; and as such, it will be judged of in history, when time shall have allowed a calm and unprejudiced opinion to be formed.

Published by

Facsimile Publisher
Ashok Vihar, Delhi-110052 (India)
Website: www.facsimilepublisher.com

Distributed by

Gyan Books Pvt. Ltd.
5, Ansari Road, Daryaganj, New Delhi-110002 (India)
E-mail: books@gyanbooks.com, Website: www.gyanbooks.com

2 222000 014117